KV-117-326

List of resources on the CD-ROM

The page numbers refer to the teacher's notes provided in this book.

INTRODUCTION

This book and CD-ROM support the teaching and learning set out in the QCA Scheme of Work for science in Year 3. The CD provides a large bank of visual and aural resources. The book provides teacher's notes, background information, ideas for discussion and activities to accompany the CD resources, along with photocopiable pages to support the teaching. All have been specifically chosen to meet the requirements for resources listed in the six QCA units for Year 3. Some additional resources and ideas have also been included to enable teachers to develop and broaden these areas of study if they wish. These include poems, simple and more complex information texts, and sheets to help children clarify their thinking or record what they find out.

The resources and activities are not intended to provide a structure for teaching in themselves, but are designed to give a basis for discussion and activities which focus on the knowledge, skills and understanding required by the National Curriculum for science. Some of the ideas build on the National Curriculum requirements and help to broaden the children's experiences.

The children are encouraged to develop skills such skills as observing, questioning, describing, sorting, sequencing, finding out, speaking, listening, reading, writing and drawing.

Links with other subjects
Maths
Skills such as counting, measuring, matching, ordering and sequencing are essential to both science and maths. Some activities, such as surveying what pets eat, using the data to make a graph and interrogating the graph to find out which pet food is the most popular, help children begin to understand the need for careful data handling. Measuring skills are fostered when children follow recipes, and they learn to use a force meter to measure the force needed to stretch different springs to the same length. Work on shadows and sundials helps children develop an understanding of how time is measured.

Literacy
There are a number of close links between the units covered in this book and work on literacy. The discussion activities contribute directly to the requirements for speaking and listening. Some of the poems and information sheets could be used in shared reading during the Literacy Hour, or to provide a stimulus for shared, guided or independent writing. There is considerable opportunity for the children to develop their independent writing skills as they produce leaflets or diaries or write simple poems using the word cards. Pictures from the CD could be printed to stimulate independent writing, or to illustrate it.

Art and design
Many of the activities suggested in the teacher's notes encourage children to use art and design to extend their understanding of a particular concept. For example, making a close, coloured observational drawing of a small area of the surface of a piece of rock, encourages children to observe fine detail and to appreciate the subtle colourings in nature. Making clay pots and sculptures from twisted wire help children to develop a 3-D aspect to their work and encourages artistic expression.

History
Children learn that some things have developed over very long periods when they study the part sundials have played in the measuring of time, and how such measurements have needed to become ever more accurate to meet the demands of modern living. Learning about the building of canals and how they were used to transport heavy goods gives children an insight into one aspect of life in Victorian times as well as helping them understand how materials are used according to their specific properties.

Geography
Examining rocks and soils from different areas, and the uses made of them, leads to an appreciation of the variety of landscapes to be found in their own and contrasting areas.

HOW TO USE THE CD-ROM

Windows NT users
If you use Windows NT you may see the following error message: 'The procedure entry point Process32First could not be located in the dynamic link library KERNEL32.dll'. Click on **OK** and the CD will autorun with no further problems.

Setting up your computer for optimal use
On opening, the CD will alert you if changes are needed in order to operate the CD at its optimal use. There are three changes you may be advised to make:

Viewing resources at their maximum screen size
To see images at their maximum screen size, your screen display needs to be set to 800 x 600 pixels. In order to adjust your screen size you will need to **Quit** the program.

If using a PC, open the **Control Panel**. Select **Display** and then **Settings**. Adjust the **Desktop Area** to 800 x 600 pixels. Click on **OK** and then restart the program.

If using a Mac, from the **Apple** menu select **Control Panels** and then **Monitors** to adjust the screen size.

Adobe Acrobat Reader
To print high-quality versions of images and to view and print the photocopiable pages on the CD you need **Adobe Acrobat Reader** installed on your computer. If you do not have it installed already, a version is provided on the CD. To install this version **Quit** the 'Ready Resources' program.

If using a PC, right-click on the **Start** menu on your desktop and choose **Explore**. Click on the + sign to the left of the CD drive entitled 'Ready Resources' and open the folder called 'Acrobat Reader Installer'. Run the program contained in this folder to install **Adobe Acrobat Reader**.

If using a Mac, double click on the 'Ready Resources' icon on the desktop and on the 'Acrobat Reader Installer' folder. Run the program contained in this folder to install **Adobe Acrobat Reader**.

PLEASE NOTE: If you do not have **Adobe Acrobat Reader** installed, you will not be able to print high-quality versions of images, or to view or print photocopiable pages (although these are provided in the accompanying book and can be photocopied).

QuickTime
In order to view the videos and listen to the audio on this CD you will need to have **QuickTime version 5 or later** installed on your computer. If you do not have it installed already, or have an older version of **QuickTime**, the latest version is provided on the CD. If you choose to install this version, **Quit** the 'Ready Resources' program.

If using a PC, right-click on the **Start** menu on your desktop and choose **Explore**. Click on the + sign to the left of the CD drive that is entitled 'Ready Resources' and open the folder called 'QuickTime Installer'. Run the program contained in this folder to install **QuickTime**.

If using a Mac, double click on the 'Ready Resources' CD icon on the desktop and then on the 'Acrobat Reader Installer' folder. Run the program contained in this folder to install **QuickTime**.

PLEASE NOTE: If you do not have **QuickTime** installed you will be unable to view the films.

Menu screen
▶ Click on the **Resource Gallery** of your choice to view the resources available under that topic.
▶ Click on **Complete Resource Gallery** to view all the resources available on the CD.
▶ Click on **Photocopiable Resources (PDF format)** to view a list of the photocopiables provided in the book that accompanies this CD.
▶ **Back**: click to return to the **opening screen**. Click **Continue** to move to the **Menu screen**.
▶ **Quit**: click **Quit** to close the menu program and progress to the **Quit screen.** If you quit from the **Quit screen** you will exit the CD. If you do not quit you will return to the **Menu screen**.

Resource Galleries
▶ **Help**: click **Help** to find support on accessing and using images.
▶ **Back to menu**: click here to return to the **Menu screen**.
▶ **Quit:** click here to move to the **Quit screen** – see **Quit** above.

Viewing images

Small versions of each image are shown in the Resource Gallery. Click and drag the slider on the slide bar to scroll through the images in the Resource Gallery, or click on the arrows to move the images frame by frame. Roll the pointer over an image to see the caption.

▶ Click on an image to view the screen-sized version of it.
▶ To return to the Resource Gallery click on **Back to Resource Gallery**.

Viewing videos

Click on the video icon of your choice in the Resource Gallery. In order to view the videos on this CD, you will need to have **QuickTime** installed on your computer (see 'Setting up your computer for optimal use' above).

Once at the video screen, use the buttons on the bottom of the video screen to operate the video. The slide bar can be used for a fast forward and rewind. To return to the Resource Gallery click on **Back to Resource Gallery**.

Listening to sound recordings

Click on the required sound icon. Use the buttons or the slide bar to hear the sound. A transcript will be displayed on the viewing screen where appropriate. To return to the Resource Gallery, click on **Back to Resource Gallery**.

Printing

Click on the image to view it (see 'Viewing images' above). There are two print options:

Print using Acrobat enables you to print a high-quality version of an image. Choosing this option means that the image will open as a read-only page in **Adobe Acrobat** and in order to access these files you will need to have already installed **Adobe Acrobat Reader** on your computer (see 'Setting up your computer for optimal use' above). To print the selected resource, select **File** and then **Print**. Once you have printed the resource **minimise** or **close** the Adobe screen using — or **X** in the top right-hand corner of the screen. Return to the Resource Gallery by clicking on **Back to Resource Gallery**.

Simple print enables you to print a lower quality version of the image without the need to use **Adobe Acrobat Reader**. Select the image and click on the **Simple print** option. After printing, click on **Back to Resource Gallery**.

Slideshow presentation

If you would like to present a number of resources without having to return to the Resource Gallery and select a new image each time, you can compile a slideshow. Click on the **+** tabs at the top of each image in the Resource Gallery you would like to include in your presentation (pictures, sound and video can be included). It is important that you click on the images in the order in which you would like to view them (a number will appear on each tab to confirm the order). If you would like to change the order, click on **Clear slideshow** and begin again. Once you have selected your images – up to a maximum of 20 – click on **Play slideshow** and you will be presented with the first of your selected resources. To move to the next selection in your slideshow click on **Next slide**, to see a previous resource click on **Previous slide**. You can end your slideshow presentation at any time by clicking on **Resource Gallery**. Your slideshow selection will remain selected until you **Clear slideshow** or return to the **Menu screen**.

Viewing on an interactive whiteboard or data projector

Resources can be viewed directly from the CD. To make viewing easier for a whole class, use a large monitor, data projector or interactive whiteboard. For group, paired or individual work, the resources can be viewed from the computer screen.

Photocopiable resources (PDF format)

To view or print a photocopiable resource page, click on the required title in the list and the page will open as a read-only page in **Adobe Acrobat**. In order to access these files you will need to have already installed **Adobe Acrobat Reader** on your computer (see 'Setting up your computer for optimal use' above). To print the selected resource select **File** and then **Print**. Once you have printed the resource **minimise** or **close** the Adobe screen using — or **X** in the top right-hand corner of the screen. This will take you back to the list of PDF files. To return to the **Menu screen**, click on **Back**.

TEETH AND EATING

Content and skills

This chapter links to Unit 3A, 'Teeth and eating', of the QCA Scheme of Work for science at Key Stage 2. The Teeth and Eating Resource Gallery on the CD-ROM, together with the teacher's notes and photocopiable pages in this chapter, can be used when teaching this unit.

As with the QCA Scheme of Work, this chapter encourages children to think about their teeth, the relationship between teeth and diet, and the importance of dental care. It also reinforces and extends their knowledge and understanding of the need to eat a balanced diet, taking responsibility for their personal health and caring for themselves.

The teacher's notes contain background information about the resources and include ways of using them as a whole class, for group work or as individuals. Some of the activities link with other areas of the curriculum, such as maths, art, English and PSHE. Wherever possible, the activities encourage the children to ask questions and develop an enquiring approach to their learning.

Resources on the CD-ROM

There is an illustration showing the various types of teeth and a diagram giving a cross section of a tooth. A photograph of an open mouth shows an example of how decay can affect teeth. A photo of a child's mouth shows a gap in the front teeth. There are photographs of groups of foods, such as meat, fish, butter and fats, bread, fruit cake and sticky/sponge cakes, sweets, fizzy drink, fruit squash, fruit, vegetables, milk and cheese. Foods such as different forms of pasta, a variety of rice grains, more unusual vegetables, and breads from other cultures are also depicted. Pictures of cat food, bird food, rabbit food and fish food are also included to indicate that other animals have similar needs to humans.

A video interview with a dentist could be used to reinforce children's understanding of how to care for their teeth.

Photocopiable pages

The photocopiable pages in the book are also provided in PDF format on the CD-ROM and can be printed from there. They include:
▶ word cards containing essential vocabulary for the unit
▶ information sheets on food groups
▶ a recipe
▶ an exercise on animal dentition
▶ a poem
▶ a game board.

Science skills

Skills such as observing, questioning, discovering, describing, sorting, sequencing, listening, speaking, reading, writing and drawing are all involved in the activities suggested for the unit. For example, looking closely at the various types of teeth and discussing their functions fosters observation and speaking and listening skills; finding out what constitutes a balanced diet, why it is necessary to eat a balanced diet for health, and writing questions to ask a visitor help questioning and writing skills. There are also activities that require the children to conduct a survey and make a graph of the results, using mathematical skills. For some activities, it may be necessary for the children to use additional reference material, allowing them to develop their research techniques and skills in using indexes and contents pages.

NOTES ON THE CD-ROM RESOURCES

FOODS

Meat counter, Fish counter, Dairy produce, Cake display, Bread, Fruit, Vegetables

It is important that children understand the need for a varied and adequate diet and the part it plays in helping them to grow and stay healthy. This collection of photographs shows foods grouped into identifiable categories and will help children to understand the wide range of foods that make up a balanced diet.

The foods shown can be grouped into the broad categories of meat, fish, fats, sugars, starches, fruit and vegetables. Children will also need to begin to understand that different food types are needed for different purposes. Broadly speaking, meat and fish provide proteins for growth and repair of body cells; fruit and vegetables provide vitamins to keep the body healthy; fats, sugars and starches give energy. If too much of this latter type of food is eaten, it is stored as fat.

Discussing the photographs

▶ Remind the children of the importance of eating a balanced diet. Stress the meaning of balance in this context: eating a variety of foods and not too much nor too little of any one type. Gauge the children's existing knowledge and understanding by asking them to suggest some foods needed for a balanced diet.

▶ Talk about the word *diet*. Many children, and some adults, think of a diet as an eating programme that you go on to lose weight, and do not equate it with what we eat normally, every day.

▶ Look at each of the pictures in turn (you could use the CD's slideshow function to facilitate this) and identify the food group and some of the foods in it. Establish what the foods in each group do for us. For example, foods such as meat and fish are good sources of protein and fats, so help to build our bodies and muscles. They are very good for our brains. Sweets and cakes give us immediate energy by increasing the amount of sugar in our blood. Fruits and vegetables give us a range of vitamins and minerals that help our general health and our skin, hair and eyes. Cereal-based foods, such as bread and pasta, provide fibre, and starches that give longer-term energy.

▶ Talk about the fact that we really need to eat some things from every food group every day, and that no food is bad for us as long as we don't eat too much of it. Explain that we should eat more of some foods, such as fruit and vegetables, than others, such as crisps and chips, to keep us healthy. Tell the children that it is recommended that we eat at least five portions of different fruit and vegetables every day.

▶ Tell the children that some people are vegetarian or vegan, and explain what these terms mean. Explain that their diets are different and that they eat things such as pulses (lentils and chickpeas for example) and soya products instead of meat and fish and, in the case of vegans, eggs and dairy products. If appropriate, encourage vegetarians or vegans in the class to share details about their diet.

Activities

▶ Ask the children to work together in groups to examine each photograph and identify as many different examples of food groups as they can. Ask them to list more foods in each group on photocopiable page 19.

▶ Let the children design balanced meals for a typical day, making sure that the recommended five portions of fruit and vegetables are included, as well as some foods from all the other food groups. If the children are divided into seven groups, they could produce suggested meals for a week and combine these to make an illustrated class menu booklet.

▶ Ask the children to design a menu of balanced meals for a day for people who are vegetarian or vegan.

Photograph © Photodisc via Soda

▶ Use cooking sessions to produce some of the dishes in the class menu booklet.
▶ Let the children look up the word *diet* in a dictionary and discuss the different meanings.

FOODS FROM OTHER CULTURES

Pasta, Rice, Vegetables from different cultures, Breads from different cultures

Some children may eat foods regularly without realising that they originally come from a variety of cultures. For example, pasta, which originates from the Mediterranean area, has become almost a staple food in Britain. All these different foods add interest and variety to a good diet. The vegetables shown are: aubergine, squash, sweet potatoes, okra, ginger and garlic. The breads shown are (left to right): pitta, naan, tomato focaccia, chapatti and tortilla.

When letting the children taste any foods, be aware of any allergies and cultural/religious restrictions.

Discussing the photographs

▶ Look at each photograph and ask the children to identify the different groups. Encourage any children who recognise individual foods (spaghetti, wild rice, aubergine, naan and so on).
▶ Consider the region of origin for each of the foods: pasta from Italy, rice from Asia, okra from north-east Africa, tortilla from Mexico.
▶ Talk about the fact that although most of us eat a wide range of foods these days, some people eat more of certain foods that are typically part of their culture and are found in the countries their families originally came from. Foods that are familiar to most children may also be prepared in very different ways in different households.
▶ Do all the children recognise everything in the pictures? Have they tried all the different vegetables? Can they name them? Do they know how they can be prepared and any dishes in which they are used?

Activities

▶ Bring in a few samples of the different foods for the children to examine.
▶ Ask the children if they know the main ingredient of most pasta and bread (wheat) and to which food group they belong (cereals).
▶ Cook using some of the foods – for example, pasta with a simple vegetable sauce. You could select a dish from the children's menus from previous activities if appropriate. Go through the ingredients with the children to demonstrate how the meal contributes to a balanced diet.
▶ Talk about one or two ingredients that are the least familiar to the class and invite a family member from a particular cultural group to cook with the children. Ask children to write out and illustrate the recipe he or she uses to add to the class book.
▶ Visit a supermarket and look for foods from a variety of cultures, including things such as ready meals (often Italian, Indian or Chinese dishes), tinned and preserved foods. Take some fruits and vegetables back to the classroom to try, including those mainly eaten by certain ethnic groups, such as sweet potatoes, okra or plantains.
▶ Make 'Like/Dislike' tally charts when the children are tasting the different fruit and vegetables. Graph the results to find out which are the favourite and least favourite from those tasted.
▶ Put a collection of recipe books from a variety of cultures in the book corner. Perhaps let the children take them home to make particular dishes with their families.
▶ Set children the task of finding out the countries of origin for all the vegetables and breads shown in the two pictures. Ask the children to list them in two columns headed 'Vegetables from different cultures' and 'Breads from different cultures'.

PET FOOD

Dog food, Bird food, Rabbit food, Fish food

Children need to realise that all animals, including humans, have to feed in order to grow and remain active, but that some animals have quite specialised diets. For example, herbivores, such as rabbits, guinea pigs, sheep and cows, only eat plants.

Discussing the photographs

▶ Look at each photograph in turn and identify with the children which animals eat the foods in the pictures.

▶ Encourage the children to identify the types of foods shown in the 'Rabbit food' and 'Bird food' pictures. What food group does the 'Dog food' picture show?

▶ Talk about diet in terms of animals and the foods different animals eat. They don't necessarily have to eat a balanced diet as we know it, because their bodies and way of life require different things. They can often eat what we can't because they have adapted to do so. For example, many birds eat berries that are poisonous to us; dogs and cats need a much higher percentage of meat in their diet than we do.

▶ Ask the children to think about animals in the wild as well as those we keep as pets. Introduce the terms carnivore, herbivore and omnivore. Discuss the fact that some animals are omnivores like us, such as most apes, many birds, rats, pigs, and so on. Animals such as deer, horses and squirrels are herbivores and only eat vegetation (leaves, shoots and roots), fruit and seeds. Carnivores, such as lions, wolves and crocodiles, only eat meat.

Activities

▶ Conduct a survey of what the children's pets eat. Which is the most common food? Let the children use ICT to make a graph of the data.

▶ Ask some children to tell the class about their pet's diet and what its favourite food is.

▶ Find out what an unusual pet such as a snake or rat would eat. A collection of pet care leaflets from a pet shop would be a useful source of reference material.

▶ Set up a feeding station for wild birds, preferably one that can be seen from the classroom window. Include a nutritious bird pudding or bird cake. See photocopiable page 20 for a recipe.

▶ If the school does not have its own pets, you might be able to borrow one that is easy to feed and will cope with the disruption for a week (for example, a goldfish or guinea pig). Supervise the children as they care for the animal and ask them to write a care leaflet for younger children to follow.

TEETH

Set of teeth, Cross section of tooth

Children will already have some appreciation that it is important they look after their teeth since they have to last them a lifetime. They will also be finding out about the various types of teeth and their individual functions.

Discussing the images

▶ Look at the illustration of the set of teeth and ask the children to find the same types of teeth in their own mouths. (You could use small mirrors or ask the children to do this by touch.)

▶ Tell the children the name of each tooth type – incisors, canines, pre-molars and molars – and point these out on the illustration: chisel-shaped incisors at the front; pointed canines at the side; flat, bumpy molars at the back; smaller bumpy pre-molars in front of the molars.

▶ Talk about the functions of the different types of teeth, relating this to their shape and position in the jaw. For example, the incisors and canines are for slicing and cutting food and the molars and pre-molars are for mashing and grinding.

▶ Discuss the fact that humans have all types of teeth in their mouths because they are omnivores and eat all kinds of food, including meats, cereals, fruit and vegetables and so need to slice, tear, squash and grind.

▶ Look at the cross section of a tooth and point out the two main parts: the crown is the white part visible above the gum; the part under the gum is the root. Talk about the various

layers that make up a tooth: enamel, dentine and pulp, and the nerve and blood vessels within the root.

▶ If possible, find a picture of a milk tooth comparable with the cross section. How is the milk tooth different from an adult tooth? (It is generally smaller and has no proper root.) See 'Caring for teeth', below, and 'Interview with a dentist', page 13, for more discussion on milk teeth.

Activities

▶ Ask the children to look in a friend's mouth to see the different types of teeth, then name them and tell each other what they are for.

▶ Ask the children to draw labelled pictures of each kind of tooth. Encourage them to add a few sentences to each picture saying where they are found in the mouth and what their functions are.

▶ Make a large copy of the tooth cross section to make a wall display. Ask children to label the various layers, using the word cards on photocopiable page 17 to help.

▶ Allocate the children research tasks to find out about the differences between the teeth of carnivores, such as lions and sharks; omnivores, such as humans and bears, and herbivores, such as cows, rabbits, sheep and horses. Tell the children to use photocopiable page 21 'Herbivore, omnivore or carnivore?' to record some of their results.

CARING FOR TEETH

Child with gap in teeth, Teeth showing decay

Children need to understand that humans have two sets of teeth and that the second set, their adult teeth, need to last the rest of their lives. In order to make sure that teeth remain healthy, children should know that they have to be looked after properly and what problems they are trying to avoid.

The discussion will need to be handled sensitively because there may be children in the class who don't have their own toothbrush or clean their teeth at all regularly.

Discussing the images

▶ Remind the children of the importance of dental hygiene and visiting the dentist.

▶ Look at the photograph of the boy showing the big gap in his top front teeth. See if the children can tell you what has happened to the missing teeth. Talk about milk teeth being smaller, temporary teeth, which last until the second, or adult, teeth have developed in the gums. When a child is about six years old, the milk teeth are shed leaving room for the bigger, second teeth to erupt. We have more adult teeth than milk teeth so that we can chew a wider variety of foods. Stress the need to care for these teeth since they have to last for the rest of their lives.

▶ Look at the child's bottom front teeth and point out that the adult teeth are beginning to grow. Emphasise the fact that our adult teeth need careful looking after both through hygiene and a healthy diet.

▶ Encourage the children to suggest how people should care for their teeth and gums and what constitutes a healthy diet, particularly in terms of tooth care. (See also 'Food and teeth', on page 12.) Mention that it is not a good idea to eat after we have cleaned our teeth before bed.

▶ Focus on the picture of 'Teeth showing decay'. Ask the children to tell you what they can see has happened to decayed teeth. (They discolour and become misshapen, look 'rotten'.) Tell the children that even if we look after our teeth carefully we can sometimes get some decay. Explain that regular visits to the dentist should stop decay getting worse.

Activities

▶ Ask the children to label the photographs with words from the word cards on photocopiable pages 16 and 17.

▶ Let the children write an imaginative story about the tooth fairy, including what the tooth fairy might do with the teeth once he/she has collected them. (Building fences, recycling them, sculptures, cobble fairy streets, and so on!)

▶ If possible, invite a dentist or dental hygienist into the classroom to demonstrate how to care for teeth, and view the video 'Interview with a dentist' provided on the CD.

▶ Ask the children to write a set of instructions on dental care for younger children.
▶ Read the poem on photocopiable page 22 to reinforce in a more light-hearted way the dangers of lack of tooth care.
▶ Ask the children to look at their toothpaste at home and note any information about what the toothpaste does that helps care for teeth (for example, it helps prevent decay). Ask some of the children to read out what they have found out from their toothpaste tube. Do they all say the same thing?

FOOD AND TEETH

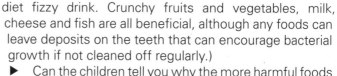

Sticky cake, Sweets, Non-diet fizzy drink, Fruit squash, Apples, Oranges, Carrots, Celery, Milk, Fish, Cheese

Children often think that sweets and sticky foods should not be eaten at all for the sake of our teeth. They need to understand that these foods can be eaten in moderation so long as teeth are looked after carefully and cleaned regularly. Children will be looking at a range of foods to see how diet can affect teeth.

Fizzy drinks and fruit squashes often contain a lot of sugar that sticks to the teeth and encourages bacterial growth. Fruits such as oranges contain acid, which can damage the enamel on our teeth, but they are also rich in vitamins which are good for us. A drink of water after eating an orange can help to wash away the potentially harmful acid. Teeth should not be cleaned immediately after eating, since acids in food soften the enamel and brushing then can damage it. Apples, carrots, celery and other crunchy fruit and vegetables help to massage the gums which helps to keep our teeth healthy. There is no substitute for regular cleaning, however, since these fruits also contain acids which can damage teeth. Milk, fish, eggs and other dairy products are rich in calcium which is essential for strong teeth and bones.

Discussing the photographs

▶ Remind the children that no foods should be banned because they are bad for the teeth, but some foods are more harmful than others, particularly if we eat too much of them or don't clean our teeth regularly and thoroughly.
▶ Ask the children which types of foods are considered bad for teeth. (Sugary and acidic foods.)
▶ Look at all of the photographs in turn and ask the children to distinguish between those foods that are more or less harmful to the teeth. (More harmful: sticky cake, sweets, non-diet fizzy drink. Crunchy fruits and vegetables, milk, cheese and fish are all beneficial, although any foods can leave deposits on the teeth that can encourage bacterial growth if not cleaned off regularly.)

▶ Can the children tell you why the more harmful foods might be more damaging? (Sweet, sticky foods stick to the teeth and particularly in the crevices between the teeth and the teeth and the gums. This provides an ideal growing medium for bacteria which cause tooth decay and gum disease.)

Activities

▶ Ask the children to sort the photographs into foods that are more or less damaging to the teeth.
▶ Brainstorm lists of foods that are more or less harmful for teeth. Make sure the lists include different foods and drinks from the ones shown in the photographs. Ask the children to tell you why they are suggesting a particular food or drink.
▶ Ask groups of children to make a poster about eating for the health of your teeth.
▶ Play the 'Tooth track' game on photocopiable page 23. This will help to reinforce what the children have been learning about caring for their teeth.
▶ Ask the children to list all the foods and drink in a favourite meal and indicate which foods are better and which are less good for the teeth.

INTERVIEW WITH A DENTIST

Video: Interview with a dentist

Discussing the video

▶ Watch the video, and tell the children to listen carefully as you will be asking questions about it later.

▶ Ask the children how many of them go to the dentist for a regular check-up. How often do they go? How often should they go? What happens when they go?

▶ Can the children tell you why dental health and care is important?

▶ Ask them what they should do at home to keep their teeth healthy.

▶ What sort of toothbrush should they use when brushing their teeth? How much toothpaste?

▶ Why is diet also important for healthy teeth?

▶ Why do we lose our milk teeth?

▶ Why did the dentist in the film want to become a dentist? Do any of the children want to be a dentist?

Activities

▶ Ask the children to make a poster about visiting the dentist to encourage everyone to go regularly.

▶ Help the children to write and act out a short play about a visit to the dentist.

▶ Make a collection of toothpaste packaging. Ask the children to find out from the boxes what the various toothpastes contain. Are they all made from similar ingredients? Do they all contain fluoride? The children could research the origins and uses of fluoride.

▶ In groups, discuss the claims on the toothpaste packaging. Does it really make your teeth 'whiter than white'?

▶ Ask the children to write a short piece about why it is good to visit the dentist regularly.

NOTES ON THE PHOTOCOPIABLE PAGES

Word cards PAGES 16–18

These cards contain some of the basic and more advanced vocabulary for the children to learn and use when looking at teeth and eating. They include:

▶ words associated with food groups and diets, such as *vegetables, omnivore, vegetarian*

▶ the types of teeth, such as *incisor, molar* and so on

▶ words related to different parts of teeth, such as *enamel, nerve, crown, root.*

Read through the word cards with the children to familiarise them with the key words of the unit. Ask which words the children have heard before and clarify any they don't understand.

Activities

▶ Shuffle the cards and spread a set of cards on each group's table. Ask the children to find specific words you call out.

▶ Use the cards as a word bank to help the children label pictures and to help them with longer pieces of writing.

Food groups PAGE 19

This sheet contains information about different food groups presented in simple tables. It lists some of the foods in each group and gives the children the opportunity to add more of their own.

Discussing the sheet

▶ Read through the sheet with the children and discuss the information contained on it.

▶ Talk to the children about the differences between the food groups and remind them of what they have already learned.

▶ Discuss why we need some proteins and fats, for example, and why we should limit our intake of high-energy foods.
▶ Ask the children to suggest additions to each group.

Activities
▶ Ask the children to complete the sheet by adding more foods to each group.
▶ Let the children tell each other in groups what they have put on their sheets. Then discuss as a class any interesting differences.

Bird cake
PAGE 20

The children can use this sheet to make a bird pudding to hang out for the wild birds and observe them feeding. The ingredients (for example, the large amount of fat, a high energy food) will help the children appreciate differences between our dietary requirements and those of other animals.

Make sure you have all the ingredients and equipment ready and arrange additional adult help. Ask the children to help you choose a suitable site for the feeder.

Discussing the recipe
▶ Talk about the needs of wild birds, particularly during the winter months when food is hard to come by.
▶ Discuss how they need a regular supply of nutritious food to maintain their body temperature and health, especially when the weather is cold and wet.
▶ Read the recipe through with the children before they begin, to make sure they understand the process. Remind them about the safety issues involved.

Activities
▶ Make the cake according to the recipe. Choose a suitable place to hang it. Observe any visitors and keep a record. Be patient, as it sometimes takes a while for the birds to find the cake. You could make more than one cake, perhaps using different hangers, and place them in different areas, which may lead to interesting contrasts in the observations made.
▶ Examine the photograph of 'Bird food' provided on the CD and talk about what these birds are eating. (Different seeds; large nuts, probably peanuts; a similar fat-based bird cake.) Ask the children if they have bird feeders at home. What do they put in them? Do they know which birds come to visit? (The birds in this picture are siskins.)
▶ Ask the children to find out what different types of food birds like to eat. Do they all eat the same thing? Are all birds herbivores?

Photograph © Photodisc, Inc

Herbivore, carnivore or omnivore?
PAGE 21

This worksheet contains diagrams of skulls of animals showing different dentitions. It will help children to understand that animals' teeth have developed according to what they eat and that different animals eat different things and therefore have different assortments of teeth.

Discussing the text
▶ Talk about different types of diet and whether all animals eat the same things.
▶ Ask whether humans are herbivores, carnivores or omnivores and how we could tell this from their teeth. Show 'Set of teeth' on the CD to remind the children.
▶ Look closely at the diagrams and discuss the teeth of the different animals. Explain how an animal's set of teeth can give information about its diet.

Activities
▶ Allocate the children certain animals to research. Tell them to find out what the animals eat and decide whether they are carnivores, herbivores or omnivores. Compile a class list under the three headings.

▶ Ask the children to complete the sheet by writing a short piece about the diet of each type of animal shown. You could also encourage them to label the diagram with the names of the significant teeth, for example large canines for carnivores.

▶ Let the children use dictionaries to check the definitions of the words *carnivore*, *herbivore* and *omnivore*.

Oh my teeth!   PAGE 22

This light-hearted poem, written from the point of view of an adult, is a fun way of stressing that adult teeth need to last a lifetime, but won't without proper care.

Discussing the poem
▶ Tell the children that although the poem you are about to read is funny, it still contains a serious message. Read the poem at least once and ask the children what the message is.
▶ Ask the children to tell you the ways in which the poet mistreated and neglected her teeth.
▶ What were the consequences of her neglect?
▶ Ask the children how she could have cared better for her teeth.

Activities
▶ Ask the children to write a poem in the style of the original, but with a contrasting approach: about caring for your teeth properly. For example, start

Oh, my teeth are such a fine asset,
I can chew to my heart's content,
When food comes I never say, "Pass it."
'Cause my mouth is one hundred percent.

▶ Ask the children to write a report about losing their milk teeth – the problems of having a wobbly tooth, how they felt when it fell out, what happened to it and what grew in its place.

Tooth track   PAGE 23

This simple board game should encourage children to look after their teeth and reinforce what they have learned about caring for their teeth. If possible, it is good to have an adult play the game with the children the first time round. You will need dice and counters.

Discussing the game
▶ Read through the forfeits and bonuses with the children to make sure they understand the instruction in each square.
▶ Talk about what we need to do in order to look after our teeth.
▶ Discuss why some squares give an advantage and some don't. Help the children appreciate this in terms of looking after their teeth.

Activities
▶ Let the children play the game in groups of two to four players. They could make their own counters from thick card in the shape of different teeth.
▶ Ask children to make up similar games on the theme of healthy eating.

Food groups word cards

vegetables

meat	fish

sugars and starches

fruit	fats

dairy products

protein

vegetarian

carnivore

omnivore

herbivore

◀ SCHOLASTIC PHOTOCOPIABLE

Teeth word cards

tooth
incisor
pre-molar
molar
canine
decay
bacteria
evidence

SCHOLASTIC
PHOTOCOPIABLE

READY RESOURCES ▶▶ SCIENCE

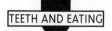

Parts of teeth word cards

enamel

dentine

pulp

nerve	**gum**

crown

cement

blood vessels

root

◖SCHOLASTIC
PHOTOCOPIABLE

Food groups

Fruit and vegetables
These are very healthy foods. It is recommended that we eat at least five portions of fruit and vegetables per day. They give us important things that we need in our diet, such as fibre, sugars, carbohydrates, vitamins and minerals.

Cabbage	Carrot	Onion
Apple	Orange	Plum
Grape	Cauliflower	Leek
Potato	Melon	

Fish, meat, eggs and dairy products
Foods from this group are also essential in a balanced diet. They help us to grow and give us mainly proteins and fats. We need less of them than fruit and vegetables. We should eat a medium amount of these.

Cod	Haddock	Shellfish
Beef	Lamb	Chicken
Milk	Eggs	Cheese

Cereals
Cereals give us mainly carbohydrates and minerals and are also essential in a balanced diet. They give us energy in a healthy way and we can eat quite a large amount of these compared to meat, fish, dairy products and high-energy foods.

Rice	Wheat	Maize

High-energy foods
These give us energy quickly. They are not bad for us unless we eat too much of them. We should only eat them in moderation.

Refined sugar	Sweets	Chocolate
Crisps		

▷ Add examples of your own to each group.

Images © Photodisc, Inc

SCHOLASTIC PHOTOCOPIABLE

READY RESOURCES SCIENCE

Bird cake

You will need
- 300g firm lard
- A handful of unprocessed, unsalted peanuts
- wild bird seed
- A saucepan
- A small bowl
- A palette knife
- A wire coat-hanger

To make the bird cake

1. Melt the lard in a saucepan over a low heat (never do this without an adult to help) until it is soft, but not see-through.
2. Remove it from the heat and allow it to cool a little.
3. Carefully pour it into the bowl.
4. Stir the peanuts and as much bird seed as you can into the lard.
5. Set it aside to harden.
6. Run a knife round the bowl and turn out the cake.

To make a hanger (three options)

A

1. Cut a square of netting (from a batch of oranges) large enough to hold the cake.
2. Place the cake in the middle and pull the net up over the sides. Tie it tightly at the top.
3. Thread a length of strong string through the net near the top.
4. Hang the cake up for the birds.

B

You will need an adult to help you with this.

1. Cut a wire coat-hanger near the hook and open it out.
2. Thread the cake onto the wire.
3. Bend up the end of the wire.
4. Hang the cake up by the hook for the birds.

C

1. Use a large skewer to thread a piece of string through the cake.
2. Tie a large knot at one end of the string to hold it in place.
3. Make a loop in the other end of the string
4. Use the loop to hang the cake up for the birds.

Images © Stockbyte; Photodisc, Inc

■ SCHOLASTIC
PHOTOCOPIABLE

Herbivore, carnivore or omnivore?

▷ Label each skull shown below with one of the words from the title. Is it the skull of a herbivore, carnivore or omnivore?

▷ Next to each each box, write about how you decided and what kind of food you think each animal eats.

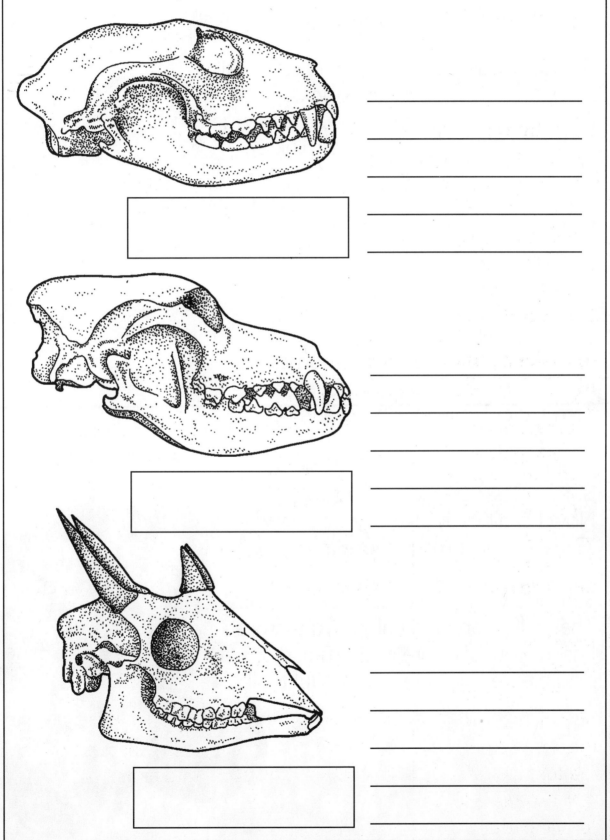

Images © Sally Alexander

■ SCHOLASTIC
PHOTOCOPIABLE

Oh, my teeth!

Oh, my teeth were such a fine asset,
I could chew to my heart's content,
But now I just have to say, "Pass it."
For tough chews these teeth are not meant.

'Twas a childhood of "Couldn't care really,"
A lifetime of sweeties and drinks.
I'd never have thought it would leave me
With a jaw full of fillings and chinks.

No truck would I have with the toothpaste,
Neglected were my pearly whites.
I'd brush in the morning with rough haste,
And sometimes not bother at night.

So my dentist he prodded and drilled,
And the rotten ones had to come out.
My sweet teeth had all but been killed.
To my diet I'd been too devout.

I could maybe afford to miss one or two,
But carelessness did it, you see:
Now I can't even take a good chew
'Cause I've lost many more than just three.

So if you want your own set of pearlies
That will gleam and enliven your smile,
Ensure you take care of them early
And please learn from my pitiful trial!

Image © Stockbyte

READY RESOURCES ▶▶ S C I E N C E

SCHOLASTIC
PHOTOCOPIABLE

Tooth track

33 Drink too much fizzy pop. Miss a turn.	32	17	16	1 Throw a 6 to start.
34	31	18 Buy fruit instead of sweets with lunch money. Go on to 24.	15	2
35	30 Dentist says teeth well cared for. Go on 4 squares.	19	14	3 Eat lots of fruit and vegetables. Move to 6.
36	29	20	13	4 Eat too many sweets. Miss a turn.
37	28	21 Eat too many sticky cakes. Go back 4 squares.	12	5
38 Miss cleaning teeth for a weekend! Go back to 25.	27	22	11 Forget to brush teeth before bed. Go back to start.	6
39	26 Brush teeth thoroughly front and back. Go on 3 squares.	23	10	7
40	25	24	9	8 Go to dentist for check-up. Have another turn.

Images © Stockbyte; Photodisc, Inc

SCHOLASTIC
PHOTOCOPIABLE

HELPING PLANTS GROW WELL

Content and skills

This chapter links to unit 3B, 'Helping plants grow well', of the QCA Scheme of Work for science at Key Stage 2. The resource gallery on the CD-ROM, together with the teacher's notes and photocopiable pages in this chapter, can be used when teaching this unit.

As with the QCA Scheme of Work, this chapter encourages children to think about what is needed for plants to grow healthily and the importance of plants as a source of food.

The teacher's notes contain background information about the resources and include ways of using them as a whole class, for group work or as individuals. Some of the activities link with other areas of the curriculum, such as maths, history, geography, art and English. Wherever possible, the activities encourage the children to ask questions and develop an enquiring approach to their learning.

Photograph © Ingram Publishing

Resources on the CD-ROM

There are pictures of food plants growing commercially in fields and greenhouses as well as on allotments. Other photographs show how certain crops are harvested – by hand, by machine or both. A photograph of a pot-bound plant shows how the roots of the plant have grown to fill the pot.

Photocopiable pages

The photocopiable pages in the book are also provided in PDF format on the CD-ROM and can be printed from there. They include:

▶ word cards containing essential vocabulary for the unit
▶ an instructional text on propagation
▶ recipes.

Science skills

Skills such as observing, questioning, describing, finding out, sorting, sequencing, listening, speaking, reading, writing and drawing are all involved in the activities suggested for the unit. For example, discovering what is needed to make a plant grow healthily will encourage investigative skills, while identifying and using plants in cooking will help children appreciate the importance of plants as a source of food. Talking about food crops will help children realise that many of the foods we eat are grown in fields or greenhouses and don't just magically appear in the supermarket! Taking cuttings and propagating plants from seeds develops their understanding of how plants grow and about their needs.

NOTES ON THE CD-ROM RESOURCES

PLANTS FOR FOOD

Wheat field, Cabbage field, Potato field, Strawberry field, Paddy field, Runner beans, Greenhouse tomatoes, Allotment

Many children may be unaware of the real source of their food beyond the shelves of their local supermarket. So much of our food is pre-washed, pre-packed or even pre-cooked, that children often don't appreciate that it was perhaps grown in a muddy field or forced into early fruiting in an artificially heated and lit green house. Children need to understand that many plants can provide food and that lots of different types of plants are specially grown for this reason.

Discussing the photographs

▶ Look at each picture and help the children to identify each crop.

▶ Mention that all the crops shown, except on the allotment, are being grown commercially: they are grown by farmers to sell on.

▶ Explain that the crops will need to be harvested and packed before being sent to a wholesaler or sold directly to a supermarket.

▶ Look at the paddy fields and explain that rice is grown in some parts of the world and is a staple food in those countries just as wheat is here. The two crops require different climatic conditions. Rice must be grown in water for part of its growing cycle.

▶ Ask the children to find some differences between the crops grown – for example, the runner beans and tomatoes grow tall and need to be supported by canes.

▶ Explain that people often grow tomatoes in small greenhouses in their back gardens but commercial growers have many large greenhouses and grow enough tomatoes to sell as a crop. (See 'Greenhouses', below.) Notice that most of the tomatoes are still green as they are not yet ripe.

▶ Sometimes, soft fruits, such as strawberries, are not sent to supermarkets or shops but are sold on a 'pick-your-own' basis. Ask the children if they have ever been to pick soft fruits. What did they pick?

▶ Look at the photograph of the allotment and discuss how some people grow plants on allotments, including vegetables, fruit and flowers for their own families. Compare the scale with commercial growers who grow much more than one family could eat.

▶ Ask the children if anyone in their family has an allotment or if they know anyone who has one. What is grown on it? Is there enough produce to share with friends?

▶ Ask the children if they have ever eaten any of the things shown in the pictures. Do they eat them just as they come from the plant or is something done to them first? Talk about how we often eat tomatoes as they come, but wheat is usually milled into flour and then baked into bread or cake or made into pasta before we eat it.

▶ Discuss how farmers need to sow the seeds and care for the plants as they grow, before harvesting the crop and sending it to market.

Activities

▶ Bring in examples of the foods in the pictures. Let the children compare the samples with the crop in the pictures. (For example, the cabbage may have had all the big outside leaves removed, strawberries may be packed in punnets without any leaves, and potatoes will have had all the plant leaves removed and may be washed and bagged. Talk about why this has been done and who has done it, to help distinguish between the growing plant and the certain part of the plant (often the fruit or the root) that we use for food.

▶ Arrange a visit to a local allotment or market garden so that the children can see crops growing in fairly large quantities.

▶ List the crops shown growing on the allotment. If you visited an allotment, was any of the same produce grown there?

▶ Ask the children to make a plan of their garden or any other garden belonging to friends or family, and mark on it any crops (either fruit or vegetables) and also any flower beds. What vegetables, or food produce like herbs, are most commonly grown?

▶ Visit a local greengrocer or supermarket to see the range of produce available. How many different varieties of potatoes, apples or cabbages can the children find?

▶ Look at the labels on the shelves and any packaging to find out where the food originates. Back in the classroom, find the countries of origin on a map or globe.

▶ Demonstrate using a mortar and pestle or two large flat stones to show how wheat can be ground into flour.

▶ Use the crops shown to make different dishes in cookery sessions. For example, make bread or cakes from flour (see photocopiable pages 32 and 33), make coleslaw, bake jacket potatoes or make mashed potato nests and fill them with baked beans. Strawberry shortcake makes a few strawberries go a long way, or make strawberry jam. Chocolate Crispy Crunchies (photocopiable page 34), using puffed rice cereal or corn flakes, are sure favourites and help children to appreciate the versatility of crops like rice. Tomatoes can be served in many ways, from soup to sauces to sandwiches.

▶ Ask the children to find out about other plants that are grown commercially for food. Which can be eaten as they are and which need to be processed before we can eat them?

GREENHOUSES

Commercial greenhouse, Garden greenhouse

Plant growth is affected by temperature. As well as water and light, plants need warmth to grow healthily. Different plants require different degrees of warmth, which is why different crops have their own growing seasons. These days, there is less evidence of this seasonal growth in the shops, as produce can be air-freighted into this country from abroad.

Greenhouses have been used for a long time to extend growing seasons by providing the warmth needed for growth. This is why many crops, such as salad vegetables, are grown under glass. In earlier times, before tropical fruits could be air-freighted into the country, 'hot houses' meant wealthy families could enjoy exotic fruits from their own gardens.

Discussing the photographs

▶ Look at the photograph of the greenhouse in a domestic back garden. Ask whether any of the children have a greenhouse in their own garden or in the garden of somebody they know. What is grown in it? What does it feel like inside when the sun is shining?

▶ Talk about why crops are grown in greenhouses. Explain that the heat from the Sun passes through the greenhouse glass and warms the air inside. The glass also helps to keep the heat in. Most commercial greenhouses are heated by large boilers and pipes in cold weather so that the growing season can be extended. Some also have lights on all night to 'fool' the plants into growing as if it were summer.

▶ Talk about the advantages of prolonging the growing season of crops as well as being able to grow crops in this country that really prefer a warmer climate.

▶ Look at the picture of the commercial greenhouse and compare its size with the domestic one. Discuss what sort of crops may be grown in a commercial greenhouse, for example salad crops such as tomatoes, cucumbers and lettuce, and many of the cut flowers that we buy.

▶ Ask the children to consider advantages and disadvantages of growing crops under glass: the costs, pests and diseases, the possibility of a longer growing season, the ability to grow non-native plants.

Activities

▶ Plant some seeds in an open plant pot and similar seeds in one covered by a clear polythene bag. Place them next to each other in a warm place out of direct sunlight. Keep them moist and observe which germinates first.

▶ Keep two similar plants in the classroom, making sure that both are growing healthily. Put one of the plants outside in the cold and observe any changes to both plants. This activity works better if the weather outside is cold or better still, frosty. Most houseplants actually benefit from some time outdoors during the summer.

▶ Ask the children to find out about other plants that are grown under glass, such as some young or delicate flowers.

▶ Visit a commercial grower if you have one in the area. Help the children to think of some

questions before the visit, such as what crops are grown, how the greenhouses are heated, where the crops go.
▶ Make a list of all the foods eaten by the class in one day and help the children to identify those that might have been grown under glass.

HARVESTING

Wheat harvest, Tea picking, Apple picking, Potato harvest

Plants that have been grown successfully need to be harvested in order to be used as food. The care and attention to the needs of particular crops are then hopefully rewarded with a larger, more successful harvest. There is a balance between costs of growing – for example, the cost of fertiliser, spraying against disease or pests, which increases the yield – and the price that can be charged in the marketplace. Some crops are grown organically and the yield is often less, making them more expensive to buy.

Discussing the photographs
▶ Look at the picture of the wheat harvest. Talk about which crop is being harvested and show the 'Wheat field' picture provided on the CD (see 'Plants for food' on page 25).
▶ Discuss how, these days, many crops are grown in very large fields (notice how the 'Potato field' in the 'Plants for food' section continues as far as the eye can see) and are harvested by agricultural machines, some of which are huge and involve complex equipment, like the combine harvester in this picture.
▶ Tell the children that in the past, wheat was cut by scythe or sickle and arranged to dry in stooks. This was a very labour-intensive operation and the entire village would rally round at harvest time to make sure the crop was gathered in before bad weather set in. Around the middle of the 19th century, different machines were invented to cut, thresh and bale the wheat. Later, in the early 20th century, a machine was introduced that combined all three operations: the combine harvester.
▶ Look at the photograph 'Potato harvest'. Notice that there is a combination of machinery and manual work being done. Explain that, at one time, children could be given a holiday from school to pick potatoes up from the ground and put them into sacks or baskets once the harvester had turned the ground over.
▶ Look at the photographs of tea and apples being picked. Discuss why some crops still need to be picked by hand. Talk about how a machine could damage soft fruits such as strawberries. Tea is still picked by hand because only the growing tips of the tea tree are picked and this is still best done by hand. In addition, labour in the countries like India where tea grows is still relatively inexpensive and plentiful. Apples are best picked by hand because they bruise easily and damaged fruit does not keep.

Activities
▶ Experiment by growing cress in different conditions – for example, in a dark corner, in bright sunlight, some with an ample water supply, some kept dry, some cold and so on. Ask the children if they can tell you the reasons for the better crop. Use the results to conclude what conditions plants need to grow well.
▶ Harvest the healthiest cress crop and make sandwiches.
▶ Choose particular fruits and vegetables and ask children to write about where they come from and how they are grown. Find out how they are harvested. If they are grown in a different country, how are the crops transported here? Make a class information book about where crops are grown and how they are harvested.

POT-BOUND

Pot-bound plant

Plants need to be able to spread their roots so that they can take in more water and nutrients from the soil to produce healthy growth. Plants that are unable to do this often fail to thrive and eventually die. Although plants make their own food through the process of photosynthesis, they still need water and nutrients in order to do this. Children at this stage do not need to know about photosynthesis, however it is important they understand that plants do not get food from the soil but make their own using sunlight.

Discussing the photograph

▶ Tell the children that this plant has been removed from its pot. Ask them if they can tell what has happened to the plant. Why would it be better off in a bigger container? Point out how the roots have extended through the bottom of the pot and wound around themselves in search of more nutrients.

▶ Talk about how important the roots of a plant are, and that they take in water and nutrients for the plant to use in making its own food.

▶ Consider what would eventually happen if the plant had been left in the pot and not moved to a bigger one.

▶ Discuss how it is particularly important for us that food plants are kept as healthy as possible in order to grow well and provide a good harvest.

▶ Explain that healthy plants are less prone to damage by insect pests and diseases.

Activities

▶ Keep a plant in the classroom for one or two weeks and observe its growth and state of health. Carefully lift the plant from its pot and cut off the roots. Replace the plant in its pot and observe any changes over the next week. The rate of change will depend on the type of plant used. Use the words on the word cards to describe what happens to the plant.

▶ Use two pot-bound plants. Re-pot one of the plants into a larger pot and compare the progress of the two plants over the next few weeks. (Leftover spring bedding plants are often out-growing their small pots or cells and can be obtained quite cheaply at the end of the season.)

▶ Take cuttings from a plant such as fuschia or geranium and root them in water. (See photocopiable page 36.) After two or three weeks you should see tiny white roots growing from the bottom of the stem. When several roots are showing, each cutting can be planted in compost in a small pot to grow on.

NOTES ON THE PHOTOCOPIABLE PAGES

Word cards   PAGES 30–2

These cards contain some of the key vocabulary the children will use in this topic. They include:

▶ words related to plant growth and agriculture

▶ terms for parts of plants

▶ adjectives that describe the health of plants.

Read through the cards with the children and clarify any they don't understand.

Activities

▶ Use the cards as a word bank to help the children label pictures or use in other writing.

▶ Ask the children to label diagrams of plants with the 'Plant parts' words.

▶ Help the children to draw and colour healthy and unhealthy plants and use the 'Plant characteristics' cards to describe the differences.

Bread, Sponge cakes, Chocolate crispy crunchies   PAGES 33–5

These are three simple recipes for the children to follow. Children may not think of these finished foods as containing ingredients that originate from plants, but bread uses flour processed from wheat, sugar in the cake comes from sugar cane or sugar beet, chocolate contains cocoa beans, puffed rice cereal comes from rice, and corn flakes come from maize. Allowing the children to weigh and measure the ingredients themselves will enhance their maths skills.

Make sure that children know and follow safety and hygiene rules when cooking.

Discussing the recipes

▶ Talk about bread being a staple food in many cultures, but sponge cakes and chocolate crunchies are luxury foods. Ask the children to tell you if they eat bread at some time each day. At which meal are they most likely to eat it? Who eats cake every day? Ask the children to think about children who go hungry and don't even have enough bread.

▶ Read through the different ingredients listed in the recipes. Help the children to identify those that originate from or contain plants.

▶ Read through the method and explain unfamiliar vocabulary, such as to 'prove' bread.

▶ Why are the chocolate crunchies extra special? (The cereal is made from rice or corn – a staple food – but chocolate is a luxury food.)

Activities

▶ Choose one or two of the recipes to follow.

▶ Ask the children to collect other favourite recipes for a class book.

▶ Look for recipes containing plants, or ingredients originating from plants. Display recipes for both sweet and savoury foods alongside images of the plants used.

▶ Find out about the staple foods in cultures where bread is not the staple food. Why is rice the staple food in many areas of the world? Why isn't wheat grown everywhere?

▶ Share and enjoy the cakes or bread with the class. Make toast or sandwiches.

Taking cuttings

PAGE 36

This sheet provides instructions for propagating a plant such as a fuschia or geranium. By taking cuttings, children can begin to understand that new plants can be produced in different ways. Some plants do not seed well, or take a long time to develop from seed, and are better grown from cuttings. Plants known as F1 hybrids (in other words, genetically modified) are often sterile and do not set seed at all.

Plants do not actually need soil in order to grow. The nutrients are dissolved from the soil in water, and plants can be grown without soil so long as sufficient nutrients are provided. A cutting will produce roots in its search for water and nutrients. Initially the plant can produce enough energy through photosynthesis to start root growth, but would eventually fail to thrive without added nutrients. Tap water contains some nutrients.

Most children will be able follow the text without much support, but others may require more help in following the instructions. Do not leave children unsupervised if they are using knives or secateurs.

Discussing the text

▶ Read through the instructions with the children and make sure they understand what they have to do.

▶ Talk to the children about the fact that taking cuttings is another way of getting new plants without growing them from seed. This is often used by commercial growers to increase the number of plants they have for sale. A cutting will mature more quickly and will be the same as the parent plant, whereas plants grown from seed may vary.

▶ Explain to the children that the cuttings have to be handled very carefully so as not to damage them, especially once the roots have begun to grow.

▶ Talk about how the new cutting sends out roots in order to obtain water and some nutrients.

Activities

▶ Help the children to follow the instructions. Stress that they should be careful when taking the cutting to avoid damaging the shoot or the adult plant. Take care not to overcrowd the jar with cuttings. If appropriate, plan to take enough cuttings to sell on a stall at the school fair.

▶ When they are ready, let the children make drawings of the cuttings with their roots before potting them on.

▶ If appropriate, carefully label each pot with the name of the plant so that customers at the stall know what they are buying.

Plant growth word cards

greenhouse

field

warmth

temperature

soil	light
water	crop

seedlings

grown for food

SCHOLASTIC PHOTOCOPIABLE

Parts of plants word cards

leaves
stem
roots
shoot
fruit
seeds
flowers

▲ SCHOLASTIC
PHOTOCOPIABLE

Plant characteristics word cards

healthy

green

yellow

pale

thin

spindly

📖 SCHOLASTIC
PHOTOCOPIABLE

White bread

**Makes 2 small loaves
or about 18 small rolls**

Ingredients

700g strong white flour
2 level tsp salt
7g sachet fast-action yeast
450ml tepid water

Method

1. Mix the flour, salt and yeast in a large bowl.
2. Make a well in the middle and add the tepid water.
3. Mix until the dough leaves the sides of the bowl.
4. Turn the dough onto a clean, floured surface and knead thoroughly for about 10 minutes.
5. Shape into a ball and place in a large mixing bowl. Cover the bowl with a clean tea towel and leave in a warm place for the dough to rise until it has doubled in size.
6. Turn onto a lightly floured surface and knead for 2–3 minutes to knock out any air bubbles.
7. Place in well-greased loaf tins or shape into small rolls and place on a well-greased baking tray.
8. Cover with a clean tea towel and leave to prove in a warm place for approximately 30 minutes.
9. Bake at 230°C/gas mark 8 until well-risen and golden brown – about 30–40 minutes for a loaf, 15–20 for rolls.
10. Turn out and cool on a wire rack.

Image © Ingram Publishing

Sponge cakes

Makes 25–30

Ingredients
225g self-raising flour
225g sugar
225g margarine or butter, at room temperature
4 eggs, beaten
Ready-made icing for decorating

Method
1. Beat the margarine and sugar together in a large bowl until light and fluffy.
2. Add the beaten eggs a bit at a time and mix in well.
3. Sift the flour and fold gently into the mixture.
4. Place a dessert spoonful of the mixture into each paper case.
5. Bake at 190°C/gas mark 5 until golden brown.
6. Allow to cool on a wire rack.
7. When cool, decorate with icing.

◢ SCHOLASTIC
PHOTOCOPIABLE

Chocolate crispy crunchies

Makes 12–15

Ingredients
A block of dark cooking chocolate
(about 100g), broken into pieces
A large knob of butter
Cornflakes or puffed rice cereal
4 tbsp golden syrup
Sultanas (optional)

Method
1. Gently melt the chocolate and syrup in a basin over a pan of hot water (adult supervision will be needed). Make sure that no water mixes with the chocolate.
2. Add the knob of butter and mix well.
3. Add as many cornflakes or rice puffs as the chocolate will take. Make sure they are all covered in chocolate by stirring gently but thoroughly. You could add a few sultanas at this stage if desired.
4. Spoon into paper cases and leave to set.

■ SCHOLASTIC
PHOTOCOPIABLE

Taking cuttings

You will need
- A healthy plant (try geranium or fuschia)
- A small jar of water
- A sharp knife or secateurs

Later you will need some small plant pots and potting compost.

1. Look for a shoot that has no flowers.
2. Cut off a piece about 6cm long, just below a leaf joint.
3. Pull off any lower leaves.
4. Place the shoot in the jar of water. Make sure the water is topped up to keep the stem covered.
5. Place the jar in a light place, but out of direct sunlight.

After about three weeks you should see tiny roots appearing from the end of the stem.

When these roots are about 2cm long, carefully plant each cutting in a small plant pot filled with potting compost. Water them in and place them somewhere light but not too hot. Keep them damp, but be careful not to over-water them.

Watch them grow into new plants. Repot them as they outgrow their pots. You can usually see this by roots coming out of the holes in the bottom of the pot.

Images © Ingram Publishing

SCHOLASTIC
PHOTOCOPIABLE

MATERIALS

Content and skills

This chapter links to Units 3C, 'Characteristics of materials', and 3E, 'Magnets and springs', of the QCA Scheme of Work for science at Key Stage 2. The Materials Resource Gallery on the CD-ROM, together with the teacher's notes and photocopiable pages in this chapter, can be used in the teaching of these units.

As with the QCA Scheme of Work, this chapter encourages children to think about and extend their knowledge of the range of materials and their properties. The resources and activities will help children to identify the uses of some everyday materials and to give reasons for their use related to their properties. Work on magnets and springs builds on the work done in Years 1 and 2 in units 1C, 'Sorting and using materials', and 1E, 'Pushes and pulls'. The properties of magnets and the metals that are attracted to them are explored, together with the forces involved in using magnets and springs.

The teacher's notes contain background information about the resources and include ways of using them as a whole class, for group work or as individuals. Some of the activities suggested will link with other areas of the curriculum such as maths, art, English and history. Wherever possible, the activities encourage the children to ask questions and develop an enquiring approach to their learning.

Resources on the CD-ROM

The Gallery includes photographs of plastic objects that have been made to look and behave like other materials. Pictures of a range of common materials help children to link them with their properties and their uses. A variety of different types of magnets and a group of fridge magnets lead to work on what magnets are and what they do. Different springs in use help children to understand why and when springs are used and the properties that make them useful. Experimenting with elastic bands helps children to understand the properties of a material that can be stretched but returns to its original size and shape when not stretched.

Photocopiable pages

The photocopiable pages in the book are also provided in PDF format on the CD-ROM and can be printed from there. They include:
▶ word cards containing essential vocabulary for the units
▶ information texts
▶ a recording sheet on magnetism
▶ instructions for making a mangonel.

Science skills

Skills such as observing, questioning, finding out, describing, sorting, sequencing, listening, speaking, reading, writing and drawing are involved in the activities suggested. For example, discussing the properties of materials leads to an understanding of the purposes for which they are used. Finding out more from secondary sources, writing about what they have found out and handling and exploring magnets and springs helps the children begin to understand the properties of both. Using a dictionary to find definitions helps develop literacy skills. Researching the use of siege machines links to history.

NOTES ON THE CD-ROM RESOURCES

LOOKS LIKE

Erasers, Knitting yarn

The objects in these pictures are made from plastic. Plastic is such a versatile material that it can often be made to look and behave like other materials – so much so that even adults sometimes have difficulty distinguishing it from the 'real thing'. At this stage, children may need lots of help to tell the difference between, for example, a plastic and a wooden tabletop. Sometimes children equate the word *material* only with fabrics for clothing, towels, bed linen and so on. Make sure that they understand that everything is made from a type of material and that fabric is one sort of material.

Discussing the objects

▶ Ask the children what material they think each object is made from and what it is used for. Point out that they are made from plastic and that sometimes it is really difficult to tell it from the real thing.

▶ Talk about plastic as a material and why it is so useful. For example, there are many types of plastic, so it is very versatile. Durable and waterproof, it can be made rigid, flexible, transparent, opaque, coloured, thick, thin and so on. It can be moulded into any shape and is relatively inexpensive to produce.

▶ Ask the children to tell you some of the plastic things that they use every day. Some are easily recognisable as being made of plastic, such as beakers or spoons, while others are difficult to tell from the material that they are made to look like, for example desks made to look like wood, or shoes or bags that look like leather.

Activities

▶ Let the children look around the classroom and school for things that look like other materials but are really plastic. (In some cases the children will need help to distinguish them.) Ask them to list the plastic object and the material that it looks like. They could also carry out this exercise at home and look for things around the house.

▶ Collect balls of knitting and sewing yarn. Ask the children to look at the labels and sort them according to the material they are made from. Are some of them a mixture? Talk about mixtures being useful because each material in the mixture has a different property. For example, wool is warm and breathable, while acrylic is durable and helps the garment to keep its shape in the wash. (Explain to the children that fabric materials such as acrylic and nylon are types of plastic.)

▶ Look at the labels in some clothes. Are they always made from the material they look like? Are some made from plastic of some kind? Are there some mixtures of plastic materials and natural materials, for example 60% cotton, 40% polyester? Are any of the clothes made entirely from plastic materials? Make two lists of all the materials used – natural or manufactured. Are there more in one list than the other? Why do the children think this is?

▶ Read the information on photocopiable page 49 about the history of plastic. Can the children find out the names of some of the scientists who discovered the various types of plastic and the circumstances of the discoveries? Ask the children to add the names to the sheet and anything else that they can find out about plastics and their uses. Suggest that the Internet may be a good place to look.

▶ Make a collection of empty plastic containers. Ask the children to find out which type of plastic they are made from and sort them into types for recycling. (The symbol for the type of plastic is usually found on the bottom of the container.) Use the information and the symbols for the various types of plastic on photocopiable page 51 to help. Make sure that all containers are empty and thoroughly rinsed before the children handle them.

WHY USE THIS MATERIAL?

Wooden chair, Plastic bottle, Box of tissues, Woollen jersey, Metal key, Car tyre, Cup and saucer, Cotton T-shirt, Silk tie, Window

Children will begin to realise that examples of the same type of object can be made from different materials. For example, a bottle may be made from glass or plastic. In some cases, a plastic bottle is preferable because it is lighter to transport and will not break. Alternatively, a glass bottle may be preferred because it is inflexible, can be cleaned and reused or recycled, or it may be more aesthetically pleasing. Children also need to understand that the properties of particular materials make them suitable for particular objects and that at different times, one property may be more important than another. For example, glass in windows is chosen for its transparency, but glass in the front of a fire alarm is chosen so that it can be shattered for the alarm to be used.

Discussing the objects

▶ Look at the photographs with the children and ask them if they can identify each object and the material that it is made from.

▶ Talk about the wide variety of materials that we use in everyday life and the fact that they have characteristics that make them suitable for particular jobs. For example, plastic is good for bottles because it is waterproof, can be easily shaped and is light to transport; wool is warm and can be made into yarn and knitted or woven into cloth for clothing.

▶ Look at the pictures again, one by one, and ask the children to tell you why they think a particular material has been used. Can they identify some of the properties that have made it suitable for making into the object in the picture? For example, the wood used for the chair is strong, attractive and fairly easily shaped and joined. Plastic has been used for the bottle because it can be moulded easily, is light, waterproof and not breakable like glass. Paper can be thin and absorbent (as in the tissues) or thicker and stronger (as in the box). Metal is used for keys because it is strong, durable and can be moulded and shaped with precision. Car tyres (rubber) are pliable and adhere to the road surface. Clay is used for vessels because it can be moulded and then fired to make a hardwearing object. Cotton is used for clothes like T-shirts because it can be made into yarn, knitted or woven into cloth that is durable, flexible, absorbent and cool. Glass is used for windows because it is transparent, rigid and waterproof.

Activities

▶ Ask the children to take each picture and write a short sentence about why the material the object has been made from has been used. Suggest they use the word cards on photocopiable page 46 to help.

▶ Ask the children to find out the origin of each material and as much about it as possible.

▶ In discussion groups, ask the children to think of another material that could be used to make a particular object shown, and explain why it might be more or less suitable. For example, clear plastic could be used for the window, but is easier to scratch and not as rigid.

▶ Make a collection of objects made from as wide a variety of materials as possible for the children to handle and discuss. (Glass nuggets, paperweights or beads are a better idea than breakable glass objects.) Ask the children to talk about why the materials have been chosen, then sort the objects according to a particular property. Use the word cards to help and add any words that the children might come up with as a reason for sorting in a particular way. How many ways could the objects be sorted? For example, glass could be sorted as transparent or waterproof, tissues could be sorted as absorbent, opaque or flexible.

WORKING WITH MATERIALS

Steelworker

Steel was once one of the most important industries in this country, but many things that were once made from steel are now made from plastics of one kind or another – for example, many car parts, and buckets.

Steelwork was typically very hard, and people worked in extremely hot, dangerous and difficult conditions.

To make steel, iron ore has to be crushed and smelted to release iron. Other materials (including carbon) are added to molten iron to produce steel. This is poured into moulds or rolled into sheets before being manufactured into objects ranging from teaspoons to ships.

Discussing the photograph

▶ Ask the children what they think the man is doing and what material they think he is working with. (Pouring molten metal into a mould.)

▶ Ask the children if they know what *molten* means. Talk about the fact that the metal has been heated to change it from a solid to a liquid so that it can be poured into moulds to make different shaped objects. As the metal cools it solidifies again and keeps its new shape.

▶ Discuss the fact that other materials can be moulded and shaped to make objects of different shapes, and tell the children that they are going to have a go with some of them.

Activities

▶ Ask the children to look around the classroom and at home and make a list of as many objects as possible that are made from steel. Have they been moulded or shaped and joined from sheet metal? How can we tell?

▶ Let the children make sculptures out of soft, twisted wire. Talk about the characteristics of the material that make it suitable for this task. The sculptures could be covered with strips of torn paper towel dipped in cellulose paste and painted (when dry) to finish them. (Do not use wallpaper paste as this usually contains a fungicide.)

▶ Look at and handle small lumps of clay. Talk about how the material feels and how it behaves.

▶ Help the children to make small pots and leave them to dry naturally. Handle them at this air-dried stage and talk about how they have changed. If you can, fire them in a kiln. (Secondary schools or a local potter are sometimes willing to fire the children's work.) Look at and handle the fired pots. How have they changed? How is the material different? What can be done with the fired pot that could not be done with the air-dried one? (The fired pot will not return to its pliable state when filled with water.)

▶ Help the children to do some embroidery. Look at the characteristics of the fabric being embroidered. (It is flexible and its weave allows a needle to go through it.) The thread is flexible and strong.

▶ Do some batik using melted candle wax and dyes. (Make sure that the children are well supervised as melted wax can give a nasty burn.) Explain that wax is a material that can be melted and will solidify again. Ask the children to look at the way in which the fabric absorbs and is coated by the wax which, when it is solid, becomes waterproof and resists the dyes except where it is cracked.

▶ Let the children choose and find out about some other everyday material or object and how it is made. For example, a leather shoe.

VARIETY OF MAGNETS

Magnets

Children should begin to understand that there is both attraction and repulsion between magnets. There is no need yet to introduce the idea of *poles*, although if you feel they are ready you may find it easier to talk about poles rather than, for example, *the red end* and *the blue end*. Encourage the children to handle a variety of magnets, experience the attraction and repulsion between them and use the correct terminology. Some children have difficulty in distinguishing between a material that is magnetic and a magnet. At this stage, many children still think that all metals are attracted to a magnet. They should investigate as wide a range of metals as possible to develop their understanding that not all metals are attracted. A set of labelled metal samples is useful. Make sure that children do not put magnets near equipment such as computers, tape recorders or televisions, as these can be damaged.

Discussing the photograph

▶ Ask the children to remind you of what they learned about magnets in Year 1. What is a magnet and what does it do?

▶ Look carefully at the picture and tell the children that all the objects are types of magnet. Talk about the different magnets shown: ring, horseshoe, bar and ceramic bar, and tell the children that they all work in a similar way in that they attract magnetic materials.

▶ Talk about the fact that only metals, but not all metals, are attracted to a magnet. (Materials that contain iron, cobalt, steel or nickel will be attracted to a magnet.)

▶ Use the words *attract, repel, magnetic, non-magnetic, attraction* and *repulsion* in your discussion about magnets and the materials that are or are not attracted to them. You could use the word cards on photocopiable page 47.

Activities

▶ Present children with a wide range of materials and a magnet and ask them to predict and then find out which material a magnet will attract. Use photocopiable page 53 and encourage the children to choose their own additional objects to test.

▶ Let the children test a collection of labelled metal samples to find out which are attracted to a magnet. Encourage them to make predictions before testing.

▶ Make a collection of objects made from more than one material including some metal – for example, a fabric pencil case or leather shoe with a metal zip, a garment with metal buttons, a spring peg. Ask the children to predict and test which part of the object will be attracted to a magnet. Was the metal in each object attracted or not? If not, can the children say why? Expect answers such as, *The zip was attracted because it was metal* or *The buttons are metal but not the sort that is attracted to a magnet.*

▶ Use colour-coded bar magnets, the sort that have a red end and a blue end, so that the children can explore and record how they behave using the correct terminology of *repel* and *attract*. For example, if you try and put the two blue ends together, they push each other away – they are repelling each other.

▶ Ask the children to explore a range of more unusual magnets, such as circular, bead or ring, and to find out if these magnets behave in the same way as the bar magnets. Do they attract and repel each other?

▶ Give the children several ring magnets with holes in them and a wooden rod that fits through the hole. Ask the children if they can make the magnets hover above each other on the rod. Can they tell you why this is happening, using their knowledge of attraction and repulsion?

▶ Ask the children to complete photocopiable page 53 by writing definitions explaining the difference between a magnet and a magnetic material and also between a magnetic and a non-magnetic material. Let them use the word cards and dictionaries to help.

▶ Help the children to devise their own fair test to find out which is the strongest magnet – for example, working through sheets of card, or measuring the distance from which each magnet will attract a magnetic object.

▶ Let the children test things in the classroom, such as the desktop, exercise books, the door and so on, to find out what materials and what thickness of material a certain magnet will work through.

▶ Ask the children to find out about lodestone and how it was used in the past. The text on photocopiable page 52 gives some information. Can the children find out more? For example, what replaced lodestones in navigation? (The modern compass was developed.)

USES OF MAGNETS

Fridge magnets

Magnets have a variety of uses. This photograph shows magnets being used in a familiar context in the home. It is also interesting for children to know that magnets are used commercially, especially in recycling processes. Although an understanding of electro-magnets is not a requirement until Key Stage 3, children might be aware of electro-magnets (magnets that can be turned on and off) used commercially, for example to pick up and move old cars at a scrap yard, or to sort out different metals for recycling.

Discussing the photograph

▶ Ask who has fridge magnets at home. Are they there just to look attractive or do they serve a useful purpose? Remind the children of the work they did on testing magnets through materials such as paper and card.

▶ Ask the children if they can think of anywhere else that magnets are used at home or at school. (For example, in wardrobe and kitchen door catches, in loudspeakers or for picking up spilt pins.)

▶ Tell the children that magnets are sometimes used in industry to sort metal objects from other materials.

Activities

▶ Ask the children to research and write an information sheet about the everyday uses of magnets.

▶ Make a simple sorter for retrieving magnetic materials (for example in a recycling process), or make a device for picking up spilled magnetic materials (such as sewing pins).

▶ Ask the children to list some objects made from magnetic materials found in the classroom. Tell them to identify whether they have been used because they are magnetic or for some other property.

SPRINGS

Elastic bands, Retractable pens, Stapler

Exploring springs and elastic bands is a good way for children to begin to understand the properties for which these materials are used, and to experience that forces have direction and vary in strength. They need to know that when a spring is stretched or compressed upwards, it exerts a downward force on whatever is compressing or stretching it. An elastic band when stretched downwards will exert an upwards force.

Make sure that the children take care when they are using elastic bands, as when overstretched they can break and spring back painfully. Ideally children should wear goggles when investigating the stretchiness of elastic bands.

Discussing the objects

▶ Look at the picture of the elastic bands. Discuss the fact that a force can be exerted on elastic bands to stretch them round a parcel, for example, or in a catapult, and when not being stretched they will go back to their original size and shape.

▶ Look at 'Retractable pens' and 'Stapler' and ask the children if they can tell you why springs have been used for the these objects. (They are compressed or stretched when the things are operating and go back to their original size and shape so that the action can be repeated over and over again.) In a stapler, the spring is compressed when the staples are inserted. As the staples are used, the spring gradually returns to its original length, pushing the staples along and ensuring that the next one is in place and ready for use.

▶ Talk to the children about the fact that springs hold things in place and give support with flexibility, for example in a mattress or chair, and that springs can be both stretched and compressed and will return to their original shape.

Activities

▶ Allow the children to explore a collection of different elastic bands, exerting a force on them, feeling the force on their hands and watching the bands return to their original shape. Can they say whether they are using a push or a pull? Can they indicate the direction of the force? If they pull harder what happens? Can they feel and see the opposing push on their hands and fingers from the elastic band?

▶ Ask the children to find out about and list some of the uses of elastic bands and other elastic materials – for example, elastic to hold up clothes, elastic bandages to support sprains and elasticised fabric for making sports garments.

▶ Make a collection of different springs and let the children test which is the easiest to compress or stretch. Use a force meter to measure the force used to stretch different springs to the same length. Is more force needed to stretch a spring further? Is more force needed to stretch heavier springs? Compress the springs and feel the push on the hand.

▶ Help the children to devise a fair test with a simple catapult push device to propel a small ball or toy car along the floor. Ask the children to predict and find out what happens if they stretch the elastic band further before propelling the object.

▶ Ask the children to list things at home or school that use springs – for example, self-closing mechanisms for doors or secateurs.

▶ Use a Slinky on steps and surfaces of different heights. Observe how it goes back to its original shape after stretching.

▶ Devise a fair test to find out whether wide elastic bands stretch further than narrow ones. The children could hang a given weight on each band and measure and compare the amount of 'stretch'. Make sure the children wear goggles and do not stretch the bands too far.

▶ The children could make a jack-in-the-box using a folded card spring.

▶ Investigate the behaviour of various wind-up toys. Do they travel further if they are wound up more? Give each toy the same number of winds. Do they all travel the same distance? If not, can the children say why?

▶ Use photocopiable page 54 to help the children make mangonel siege machines to batter down the enemy's walls! Talk about how they work. Why are elastic bands used to supply the firepower? Why are they twisted? You could construct some simple, fairly flimsy, walls for the children to aim at.

NOTES ON THE PHOTOCOPIABLE PAGES

Word cards

PAGES 46–8

These cards contain some of the basic vocabulary for the children to learn and use when investigating characteristics of materials and magnets and springs. They include:

▶ adjectives describing characteristics of materials, such as *waterproof, flexible, transparent*

▶ words related to magnetism and magnetic materials, such as *attract, repel, steel*

▶ words related to springs and elasticity, such as *stretch, compress, force*.

Read the word cards with the children to familiarise them with the key words of the units. Ask the children which words they have heard before, and clarify any they don't understand.

Activities

▶ Spread the cards on the table and ask the children to find specific words.

▶ Use them as a word bank to help the children label pictures or to help them with their writing.

▶ Call out the names or show examples of a range of different materials, both magnetic and non-magnetic, and ask the children to hold up a magnetic or non-magnetic word card.

History of plastic

PAGE 49

This sheet gives a brief history of some of the major discoveries of various types of plastic and helps the children appreciate how plastics are a surprisingly recent development given their prevalence today. Some details, such as the names of inventors, have been deliberately omitted so the children can find these out during their research.

Discussing the text

▶ Read the text together. Discuss the types of materials used before plastics were invented.

▶ Can the children tell you why plastics have replaced these materials for making some objects? Talk about the availability and costs of some raw materials and the conservation issues surrounding materials such as ivory and hard woods. Mention that plastics, too, are derived mainly from a source that has conservation issues – fossil fuels, which will not last forever. Talk about the fact that many plastics are very durable and do not rot or decay and it is therefore difficult to dispose of them in an environmentally friendly way. Those that cannot be recycled often end up in landfill sites where they last for many, many years. Nowadays some biodegradable plastics are made.

Activities

▶ Ask the children to work in small groups to read and discuss the sheet before doing the activities. They could make an information booklet from other information they find.

▶ Orally or as a written exercise, ask comprehension questions on the text.

▶ Ask the children to find out more about how different plastics (for example, nylon) are made and used.

▶ Let them use the Internet to find out about new plastics that are being developed from renewable sources. For example, such things as starches, resins and lactic acid are increasingly being used to make biodegradable plastics for use in surgery and catering.

Using plastic PAGE 50

This information text can be used to get children thinking about the huge range of objects that are made from different types of plastic. It reminds children to think of a wider variety of objects than those that are obviously plastic. Because of its versatility and its ability to be used as a 'look-alike', plastic is often a difficult material to identify in use.

Discussing the text

▶ Read the text through together. Talk about the range of everyday objects that are made from plastic. Do any of the things mentioned surprise the children?

▶ Discuss how plastic is often made to look like a different material.

▶ Talk about the fact that the term *plastic* includes a variety of materials, some of which the children may recognise, such as PVC and polythene. Help the children notice this by comparing two objects normally referred to as *plastic* – for example, plastic bags and plastic bottles.

▶ List some of the names of fabrics that are plastic-based, such as nylon, polyester and acrylic. Look at the properties of plastic mentioned in the text that make it a good material to use in clothing/linen fabrics and carpets.

▶ Talk about some of the other objects mentioned and why plastic is used to make them.

Activities

▶ Ask the children to look at the labels in their clothes to find out whether plastic has been used in their manufacture.

▶ Look at the photographs of look-alike objects made from plastic – 'Erasers' and 'Knitting yarn'. Ask the children to look for things in their homes that are made from plastic but look like another material. Back at school, ask the children to tell you some of the things they have listed. Has anyone found anything unusual? What is the most common object?

Sorting for recycling PAGE 51

This sheet gives some information and the symbols for various types of plastic that can be recycled.

Discussing the text

▶ Help the children to read the difficult chemical names of the different plastics. Notice that they all have the prefix *poly*, meaning 'many', indicating that these are complex materials.

▶ Talk about why we need to recycle materials. Discuss the amount of waste materials put into landfill sites that could be recycled. Most of the plastic used these days does not rot or degrade, but much of it can be recycled – and the more we can recycle, the better for the environment and the longer the petrochemicals used in their manufacture will be around. Plastic drinking cups, for example, can be recycled into materials as diverse as pencils and fleece jackets.

▶ Ask the children to suggest other materials that could be recycled (for example, glass, paper, cardboard, clothing).

▶ What contribution do the children and their families make towards recycling?

▶ Does the local council encourage recycling? If so, how?

Activities

▶ Collect empty, washed out plastic containers and ask the children to sort them for recycling.

▶ Ask the children to look at all the plastic containers at home, in their kitchens and bathrooms, then note down their uses and the number in the triangle. Back at school, use the sheet to find out the type of plastic they are made from. Is a certain type of plastic always used for the same type of container?

▶ Use a large map of the locality and mark all the recycling points on it.

▶ Ask the children to find out where the nearest recycling points to home and school are, and which materials can be recycled there.

▶ In shared writing, compose a letter to the local council suggesting good places for extra points or ways of recycling waste.

▶ See if the children can work in groups to come up with ways of using fewer materials, particularly for packaging, in the first place, so that there is less that needs recycling or throwing away.

Lodestone PAGE 52

This text gives a simple explanation of what lodestone is and how it was used, and gives children the opportunity to find out more.

Discussing the text

▶ Can the children describe what a compass is used for? What group of people is most likely to use them? Establish how they are particularly necessary for seafarers because there are no landmarks for them to navigate by.

▶ Talk about how a compass works and how the magnetised pointer in the compass always points north.

▶ Read the text and talk about how lodestone was used before compasses were invented.

Activities

▶ Let the children use a compass to find out which direction from where they are is north.

▶ Encourage the children to use the Internet to find out more about lodestone and what it was used for. Compile their work into a class information book.

Magnetic or non-magnetic? PAGE 53

This recording sheet can be used throughout the children's investigations of magnetism. Encourage them to adapt or add to the list of objects to be tested. They should complete their technical definitions towards the end of their work on magnetism, when they have a greater understanding.

Making a mangonel PAGE 54

This sheet gives a detailed plan of how to make a mangonel based on a siege machine originally invented by the Greeks and improved on and developed by the Romans and in Medieval times. These early siege catapults were regularly used in battles to break down the defences of walled castles and fortified towns, before armaments like cannons replaced them. These machines used a bundle of twisted ropes or a beam under tension to propel a missile at a target. The missiles were often large rocks or tight bundles of pitch-soaked burning rags.

Discussion

▶ Give the children some of the background history to mangonels. Read through the text and explain that it shows how to make a simple toy version.

▶ Point out that the mangonel uses the spring in an elastic band to launch a missile.

▶ Remind the children that they should only use a light, soft missile when testing their mangonels. Ask them why this is.

Activities

▶ Help the children to make the mangonel according to the instructions.

▶ Test-fire the mangonel and see how far the missile travels before landing. Can the range be improved? How? Allow the children some time for tweaks and adjustments.

▶ Let groups test different machines to see which propels a missile the furthest. Make sure each machine uses the same missile to make the test fair, and test each machine several times. Create a graph of the results.

▶ Ask the children to find out as much as they can about siege machines in history; what gave them their power and how they were used.

Materials word cards

waterproof
strong
flexible
hard
absorbent
transparent

wood	glass
plastic	**metal**

◣ S C H O L A S T I C
P H O T O C O P I A B L E

Magnetism word cards

iron	steel

aluminium

copper

magnetic

non-magnetic

attract	repel

attraction

repulsion

SCHOLASTIC
PHOTOCOPIABLE

Springs and elasticity word cards

stretch
squash
compress
exerts
force
pull towards
push up on
elastic

◣ SCHOLASTIC
PHOTOCOPIABLE

History of plastic

Life without plastics would be very different for us. We are surrounded by plastic objects. Plastics are found in the fabrics we wear, the materials used in buildings, the equipment in hospitals, and things such as toys, CDs, pens, phones and computers that we use for pleasure and business.

In about 1862, a type of plastic was invented using an organic base that could be moulded and carved, but the raw material was very expensive and the plastic did not catch on.

Towards the end of the 19th century, thousands of elephants were being killed every year in order to make billiard balls from their ivory. Ivory balls were not uniform, however, and the way they played was unpredictable, so a replacement material was needed. The answer was found accidentally when a scientist spilled a bottle of collodion and saw that it congealed into a tough, flexible film. Because collodion is brittle, however, these balls sometimes shattered when they hit each other! Camphor was added to counteract this effect until further developments in plastics led to the material for modern snooker balls.

The first completely synthetic substance was developed in around 1909. A chemist made a liquid resin that came to be called Bakelite. Bakelite could be poured; it hardened quickly and took the exact shape of a container or mould. Once it was properly set, it never changed. It would not melt, burn or boil under heating, or dissolve in any common solvent or acid. These properties made it very useful. Bakelite could also be added to other materials to change their properties – it made softwood more durable, for example.

From the 1920s, plastic objects became more and more common. Nylon was invented, and this tough, versatile fibre came to replace animal bristle in brushes, silk in stockings and wool in carpets, for example.

During the 1930s, 1940s and beyond, more and more plastics were discovered that could replace supplies of natural materials that were running out. Acrylic, neoprene, polyethylene, polyvinyl chloride (PVC), vinyl, Teflon and many more came into use.

Most modern plastics are made from petrochemicals obtained from oil. Many everyday things are made from plastic, and plastics are important in advanced technologies, such as space programmes, and in medical equipment, including artificial limbs and pacemakers.

Text based on information from the American Plastics Council. Image © Stockbyte

Uses of plastic

Most modern plastics are made from petrochemicals. Petrochemicals are extracted from oil, which is a fossil fuel.

Very many things that we use today are made from plastic. Some are obvious, such as plastic bottles, carrier bags, plastic beakers, pens and computer keyboards. Others are less obvious, because plastics can be made to look like other materials.

It is likely, for example, that some of the clothes you wear are made from plastic of one sort or another. Plastic threads can be made and woven into many different fabrics, some of which look and feel very like natural materials such as cotton. Fabrics made from plastic, like polyester, nylon and acrylic, are generally easier to wash and may last longer than natural fabrics. Often, clothes are made of a mixture of plastic and natural threads, so that the long-lasting and washable properties of plastic and the softness and breathable nature of wool, for example, are combined to make a practical garment that is very comfortable to wear.

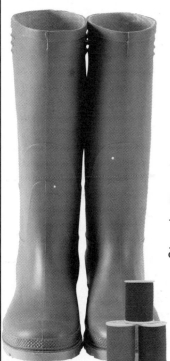

Because it is so hard-wearing, it is likely that the carpets in your school are at least partly made from plastic. Things like tabletops, cupboard doors and floor tiles are often plastic that is made to look like wood.

We sometimes think of objects like wellington boots and tyres as being made of rubber, but in fact they are made of plastic, too. Natural rubber goes sticky when it is hot, and hard and brittle when it is cold. Plastic can be made to behave like rubber without these disadvantages. Plastic really is extremely versatile.

Images © Stockbyte

Sorting for recycling

You may find these symbols on plastic containers, which mean that they can be recycled.

▷ Collect empty plastic containers, look for the symbols to identify which type of plastic they are, and sort them into groups for recycling. Use the symbols to label the boxes you store them in.

Symbol	Name	Description	Example uses
1 PET/PETE	Polyethylene terephthalate	Rigid, usually clear or green	Fizzy drinks bottles, water bottles, vegetable oil bottles
2 HDPE	High-density polyethylene	Semi-rigid, clear, or coloured and opaque	Household bottles – milk, bleach, detergent, hand lotion; margarine tubs
3 PVC	Polyvinyl-chloride	Semi-rigid, glossy	Detergent bottles, pipes
4 LDPE	Low-density polyethylene	Flexible, smooth, glossy	Bin bags, sandwich bags, can-pack rings
5 PP	Polypropylene	Semi-rigid, very slightly glossy	Buckets, tubs, screw-on lids
6 PS	Polystyrene	Stiff, can be brittle, glossy, often textured	Food trays, disposable beakers, CD cases
7 OTHER		A plastic that doesn't fit above categories, may be acrylic, melamine	Plastic plates, items using layers of different plastics

Images © Soda

◣ SCHOLASTIC
PHOTOCOPIABLE

READY RESOURCES ▶▶ SCIENCE

Lodestone

A lodestone is a special piece of magnetic rock called magnetite, an oxide of iron ore. The Chinese discovered lodestones well over 2000 years ago. They called them 'loving stones' because, being magnetic, they liked to 'kiss' and attract other magnetic objects.

Not every piece of magnetite is a lodestone. The piece has to have a particular crystalline structure. And not only this; it has been found that the stone has to have been struck by lightning to make it magnetic. The lightning, an enormous electrical discharge that lasts for much less than a second, turns the right sort of magnetite into lodestones.

Lodestones and navigation

For many hundreds of years, sailors would sail very close to the coastline so that they could always see where they were. Those that went out of sight of the land had to rely on the sun and the stars to help them to navigate. Sometimes, when they were not very good at this skill, they just disappeared!

The ancient Chinese found that if they put a small, pointed piece of lodestone on a sliver of wood and floated this on water, it always pointed in a north–south direction. They had invented the earliest compass.

▷ Find out more about lodestones. How did their use change? Who else used them to navigate? Write about what you find out.

Image © Ingram Publishing

Magnetic or non-magnetic?

▷ Predict which of these objects are magnetic. Then conduct an investigation to test your predictions.

	Prediction: magnetic (✓ or ✗)	Result: magnetic (✓ or ✗)
Paperclip		
Aluminium drinks can		
10 pence piece		
2 pence piece		
Pencil		
Pencil sharpener		
Filing cabinet		
Classroom door handle		
Teaspoon		

▷ Write your own definitions to explain what is meant by:

● a magnet

● a magnetic material

● a non-magnetic material

■ SCHOLASTIC
PHOTOCOPIABLE

READY RESOURCES ▶▶ S C I E N C E

Making a mangonel

You will need

- A wooden base board, approx 40cm × 15cm, with 2 pairs of nails in the corners at one short end and a clothes peg fixed at one opposite corner (see Fig 1)
- 3 short elastic bands of the same size
- A plastic teaspoon
- A screw eye
- Strong thread
- Ping-pong balls, paper balls or small sponge balls

1. Thread two elastic bands over opposite nails, across the width of the base. The bands should be slightly stretched. (Fig 1)

2. Twist the handle of the teaspoon between the elastic bands until they become tight. Make sure the bowl of the spoon is facing up and the spoon is able to pivot. (Fig 2)

3. Fit the third elastic band across the two end nails as a stop. (Fig 3)

4. Fix a screw eye into the base roughly level with the bottom of the spoon bowl and one pair of nails. Tie one end of a length of thread (about the same length as the teaspoon) around the handle of the spoon next to the bowl. Thread it through the screw eye and tie a bead or washer on the other end. Hold the bead in the jaws of the peg. (Fig 4)

5. Place your ammunition in the spoon and open the peg to fire! (Fig 5)

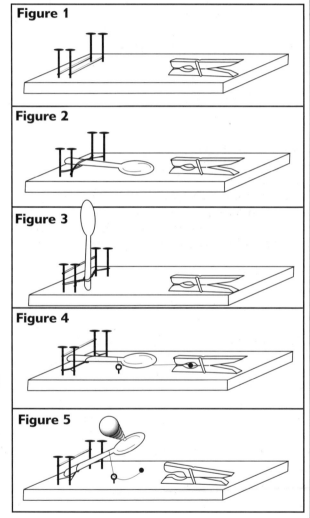

Figure 1

Figure 2

Figure 3

Figure 4

Figure 5

▶ SCHOLASTIC
PHOTOCOPIABLE

ROCKS AND SOILS

Content and skills

This chapter links to unit 3D, 'Rocks and soils', of the QCA Scheme of Work for science at Key Stage 2. The Rocks and Soils Resource Gallery on the CD-ROM, together with the teacher's notes and photocopiable pages in this chapter, can be used in the teaching of this unit.

As with the QCA Scheme of Work, this chapter helps children learn about different rocks and soils and how some of them are formed, and considers some of their characteristics and uses.

The teacher's notes contain background information about the resources and include ways of using them as a whole class, for group work or as individuals. Some of the activities link with other areas of the curriculum, such as geography, history, art, maths and English. Wherever possible, the activities encourage the children to ask questions and develop an enquiring approach to their learning.

Resources on the CD-ROM

There are photographs of different types of rock, in their natural context and as building materials, showing how some of these materials are used in our everyday environment. Photographs of different soils illustrate the variety of soil types to be found and how their composition makes a difference to the way they drain or retain water and how they are made use of by us. Images of a quarry, cliffs, a soil profile and the Grand Canyon show the layers that are formed by certain rocks. A photograph of a sculpture being formed shows how some types of stone can be shaped and carved as an art material.

Photograph © Claire Brewer

Photocopiable pages

The photocopiable pages in the book are also provided in PDF format on the CD-ROM and can be printed from there. They include:
▶ word cards containing essential vocabulary
▶ information texts on rock types and canal building
▶ a set of instructions on taking a soil profile.

Science skills

Skills such as observing, questioning, describing, sorting, finding out, listening, speaking, reading, writing and drawing are all involved in the activities suggested for this unit. For example, looking closely at samples of different soils and describing them in detail will help children realise that not all soils are the same. Close observation of rocks can raise questions about how those rocks were formed and generate greater awareness of the prevalence of rocks around us.

NOTES ON THE CD-ROM RESOURCES

NATURAL OR MANUFACTURED?

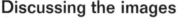
Brick, Breeze-block, Block paving, Pebbles, Slate, Gravel pile

Rocks are all around us and are used in a variety of ways, from building to jewellery. Natural stone was used as a building material for centuries, but became uneconomic as buildings became more prolific and in areas that were not close to a good supply of stone. Stone is still sometimes used, but cheaper manufactured building materials were developed, including bricks, which are more often used today. These days, it is often quite difficult to distinguish between natural materials and those that are man-made or reconstituted. For example, concrete can look very like pudding stone, which is a naturally occurring rock. Many garden ornaments that look as though they are made from a natural stone are really made from a reconstituted stone, which can be moulded into the desired shapes.

As well as identifying made materials from the natural ones, children will begin to understand how all these different rocks and made materials are used in the environment.

Photograph © Photodisc via Soda

Discussing the images

▶ Look at each photograph in turn. Can the children recognise all the materials?

▶ Identify which are made and which are natural rock. The children may guess this from the regular shape of the blocks. Talk about where these materials come from. For example, bricks are made from clay, shaped and fired in a factory; breeze-blocks are made in a factory from concrete (gravel, sand and cement), and sometimes pulverised fuel ash; while slate, gravel and pebbles are natural rocks.

▶ Discuss what each material (natural and manufactured) may be used for. Have they seen them in use anywhere? Where are pebbles, for example, normally found? What use do we make of them? (Usually decorative.) Gravel is the result of rocks being broken down by weather or water. Gravel beds are usually found in river valleys where the very small rock fragments have been washed down and deposited over many thousands of years. The picture shows gravel being extracted from one such bed. Talk about the fact that gravel comes in different sizes and is sometimes used decoratively and sometimes in construction.

▶ Some children may have experience of building work and be able to talk about some of the materials they saw being used. Did they see breeze-blocks being used?

▶ Have they noticed what their own home is made from? Is it made from brick? What is the roof made from – tiles (usually clay) or slates?

▶ What sort of materials do the children have in their gardens or in the local park? Are there gravel paths, rockeries or paved walkways? Look at the photograph of the block paving and talk about how bricks of different shapes and sizes can be used to make paths, pavements and driveways as well as buildings.

▶ Identify the materials used in the school buildings.

Activities

▶ Ask the children to sort natural materials in the pictures from manufactured ones.

▶ Look carefully at each group and compare the natural and made materials. Manufactured materials tend to be more regular in shape and have a more consistent colour and texture (the white deposits on the brick notwithstanding). Ask the children to begin two lists, one of similarities and one of differences within the groups. Encourage them to think of other rocks and made materials that could be added to the lists.

▶ Visit a garden centre and compare the material that ornaments are made from with rocks intended for rockeries.

▶ Ask the children to look around the locality for any natural materials used in building or paving.

▶ Ask the children to find out how bricks or breeze-blocks are made.

▶ If there is building work going on in the area, and if it is safe to do so, take the children to look at the materials being used and how they are used. For example, are breeze-blocks used on outside walls? Help the children to find out why not. (Breeze-blocks have lots of air spaces in the material, making them suitable for insulating internal walls. However, they are not aesthetically pleasing and are only used for external walls of buildings such as garages, farm buildings and so on, unless they are rendered with a more pleasing finish.)

EVERYDAY USES

Dry stone wall, Stone sculpture, Road building

Rocks differ in their properties, making certain rocks suitable for certain purposes. One of the main and most useful properties of many rocks is hardness. Rocks used in the hardcore that makes up the foundations of roads need to be very hard and strong to withstand the continual weight of heavy road traffic. Similarly, a soft rock would not be practical for making pavements since it would wear away quite quickly and become uneven. The stone selected to make dry stone walls was usually a stone found in the environment where the wall was built, a cheap and plentiful material to use. Slate is not an absorbent rock and can be cleaved into thin sheets, making a good roofing material. When making sculptures and carvings, craftspeople choose a stone for its aesthetic qualities as well as for how well it can be worked into the chosen design.

Discussing the images

▶ Look at the picture of the 'Dry stone wall', taken in North Wales. Remind the children of their discussions about rocks and stones used in building. Explain how in the past, important buildings were sometimes made of stone brought from other parts of the world, but 'ordinary' and more functional structures, such as cottages and dry stone walls, were built from the stones that were found nearby.

▶ Explain that the same materials are still used to make and repair dry stone walls today. Note the significant feature of dry stone walls: that no mortar is used to keep them together, unlike the domestic/commercial walls they may have seen. Only careful selection of shapes and sizes of individual stones holds them together.

▶ Look at the photograph that shows a sculptor at work. Discuss what the properties of the stone he is carving might be. (Too hard and it would be difficult to work, but too soft and the weather and pollution would wear it away quickly; if it were brittle it might be difficult to achieve desired shapes or smooth lines.)

▶ Talk about how rock is weathered over time and how the edges of, for example, very old carvings or headstones are worn away. Mention that these are probably rock like sandstone or limestone rather than more hardwearing granite or marble (which was often used for sculpture in ancient times).

▶ Discuss the fact that rock is usually waterproof although some rocks, such as sandstone and limestone, are more porous than others.

▶ Look at the 'Road building' photograph. Talk about why rocks are used to build roads and the properties that the type of rock used would need to have. Mention that the rocks shown at the front of the picture would be crushed and made smaller and compacted very tightly.

▶ Ask the children to tell you whether they have any natural rocks in their gardens, such as gravel or pebbles, or whether they have seen any in the park. Remind them that rocks may be very small – that even sand (but not coral sand) is granulated rock.

Activities

▶ Visit a local cemetery and look at the headstones. See if the children can tell which are older without looking at the dates. Look for signs of weathering and the amount of moss or lichen. Are they all made from the same sort of rock or stone? If possible, take reference materials with you and let the children find out the names of some of the rocks used. (Slate, marble and granite are the most usual types.) Ask the children to consider if different types of rock make better gravestones than others.

▶ Take the children to look at various types of building in the local environment and list the materials used in them. Do any of them use natural rocks or are they all manufactured materials? Why have these materials been used in the way they have? For example, slate is sometimes used for roofs. Being a hard, non-porous rock that can be made thin, it allows the rain to run off and keeps the building dry.

▶ Ask the children to look for things at home that are made from stone. Advise them to look for things like a marble pastry board, a rolling pin, a mortar and pestle, paperweights, hearth tiles and jewellery. Ask the children to list the properties of each stone that make it suitable for the purpose it is being used for. Go on to explain that many things in the house are made from rock even though we may not recognise it as such. For example, the plaster on the walls is made from gypsum, concrete made from rock is used for floors, and there may be sand in an egg timer.

▶ Ask the children to make a survey of building materials used to build the houses where they live. Construct a graph to find the most common materials used for walls or roofs.

▶ Make a class scrapbook of pictures of things made from stone – buildings, pavements, jewellery, ornaments and so on.

▶ Spread some sand on a piece of white paper and let the children use a hand lens or microscope to look at the individual grains. Many children may not realise that sand is made up of millions of tiny pieces of finely weathered rock. There may also be minute parts of shells and coral in the sand, depending on where it came from.

▶ Gently and carefully rub two rocks together to produce grains that indicate how sand is formed. Use a soft rock such as sandstone. (Note the name.) Is it easy to produce grains? How long would it take to fill a sand tray or sandpit?

ROCKS

Cliff, Muddy field, Pavement, Moor, Quarry, Mountain, Grand Canyon

Rock lies beneath all surfaces, even though we may not be able to see it. This selection of photographs shows mountains and cliffs, canyons and a quarry where the rocks are all quite obvious. A picture of moorland shows outcrops of rocks. Pictures of a pavement and a muddy field demonstrate how underlying rocks can be covered and hidden, although in the case of the pavement, people have covered the rock with different 'rock' of their own making.

Try to collect a selection of rocks for the classroom so that the children are able to examine different types of rock. It is better to obtain these from a known source, especially if you wish to look at the structure of a particular type, or if you wish to provide the children with contrasting types. Rocks picked up in the locality will usually be of the same type, while others may be difficult to identify. Individual rock samples should be at least fist-sized so that the children can feel the weight and texture.

Discussing the images

▶ Look at the pictures with the children and discuss what they show. Can the children tell you about any areas in the pictures where they could be in danger? Stress that they should never go into a quarry because it is a very dangerous environment. Many disused quarries or sand pits may have areas of very deep water. Also, they should only visit cliffs in the company of a responsible adult.

▶ Ask the children to describe a cliff. Where would they see one? Then look at the picture of the cliff. Point out how layers of silt and sand collected over millions of years have been pressed down to form sedimentary rock (see photocopiable page 67).

▶ Explain that pressures deep in the Earth often forced the layers to deform and over the years the wind and water have worn away softer surface materials and exposed these layers of rock in cliff faces or outcrops.

▶ Look at 'Muddy field' and 'Pavement' and talk about how we cannot always see the rocks beneath our feet because they are covered in soil (or mud) or buildings, but that there is always rock to be found if we dig down deep enough. Sometimes an area is muddy because the underlying rock is impervious (does not let water through) and stops the water draining away.

▶ Look at the 'Moor' photograph, from Yorkshire. The soil layer is very thin, so only plants with shallow roots such as heathers and myrtle are able to grow. Larger plants such as trees cannot find enough soil to anchor their roots. Explain that in some places, as in this picture, the softer top layers of soil have been worn away and we can see the rocks breaking through.

The outcrops on the Yorkshire Moors are mostly a type of sandstone. Note how the edges of the rocks have been smoothed and eroded by the weather.

▶ Show the children the picture of the limestone quarry in North Wales. Remind the children that rock is a useful material for building. In some places, people have found a high concentration of a particular rock and quarries have been created from which rock is removed by blasting and digging. Help the children to see how deep the quarry is and notice the layers of rock that were formed deep in the Earth, millions of years ago. Limestone is used as a rock for building, but most is burnt at high temperature to make the main component of cement.

▶ Look at the photograph of the mountain in a ski resort. Briefly tell the children how movements in the Earth's surface cause mountains to be formed. The Earth's crust is made up of several plates that are very, very slowly but constantly moving. Sometimes, where these plates meet, they push together and the land is forced upwards, creating mountain ranges. Demonstrate this simply by pushing on each end of a sheet of paper so that the middle rises up. The higher and more jagged the mountains are, the younger they tend to be, since older mountain rocks have usually been weathered into rounder, smoother shapes.

▶ Finally, look at the photograph of the Grand Canyon, with its maze of cliffs and smaller canyons. Talk about how the canyon was formed over million of years by erosion from water, ice, wind and the Colorado River. The sedimentary layers can be seen quite clearly. The different colours of some of the layers show how they were laid down at different times.

Activities

▶ This activity is best done outside. Fill a large plant tray with sand and gravel, and lift one end with a brick (or something similar) to tilt it. Gently pour a stream of water from a jug or watering can on the raised end of the tray. Watch how the sand and gravel is moved and worn away, creating a 'valley'. Relate this to how valleys and canyons have been formed over millions of years.

▶ Roll out a flat sheet of plasticine, clay or flour dough (making sure it is not stuck to the table). Gently and slowly push the sides of the sheet towards the middle and watch 'mountains' form.

▶ Help the children to build a rockery in the school garden, using different rocks labelled with their names or where they came from. It is not necessary for children to know the names of particular rocks, but some may be interested to find out.

▶ Ask the children to test each rock for hardness by drawing with them on the playground. Very hard rocks such as granite will make little or no mark. Soft rocks such as chalk will make very distinct marks. List them in order of hardness.

▶ Ask the children to find out how rocks are formed (see photocopiable page 67). See if the children can find out the names of some common rocks (perhaps those common to the local area) and which group they belong to.

▶ Let the children use magnifiers to look for crystals in the lumps of rock. These are usually found in igneous rocks. The rocks that cooled the slowest have the biggest crystals.

▶ Make a hole in a piece of card about the size of a two pence piece. Tell the children to place this over a piece of rock and make a detailed coloured drawing of what they see through the hole. Ask them to match the colours as closely as possible.

▶ Ask the children to write a poem about rocks at the seaside, focusing on pebbles, sand or cliffs.

▶ Ask the children to paint a landscape with prominent rocks, for example a dale, a snowy mountain scene or one including a quarry.

Photograph © Corel

SOILS

Children will begin to realise that there are many different types of soil, and that the colour and properties of the soil are often a reflection of the type of underlying bedrock. A red-coloured rock will result in a red soil, as in Devon. In South Wales, soil can be very black because of the underlying coal seams. In some areas, such as the Fens, the soil is more a result of rich materials being deposited at the bottom of shallow seas that have since drained. Different types of soil will drain at different rates. A clay soil will hold water, while a sandy soil allows water to drain away quite quickly. If possible, collect samples of soils from different areas so that the children have some to compare with the local soil.

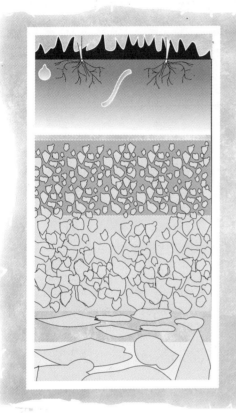

A photograph of a soil profile shows how the soil develops from the underlying rock. The top, fertile layer contains humus (organic matter), making it darker in colour than the next paler, more pebbly layer. Bigger stones come next and then, if the profile goes deep enough, the underlying rock.

Before children handle soil samples, make sure that any cuts are covered and that they wash their hands thoroughly afterwards.

Discussing the images

▶ Look at the pictures of soils and remind the children how soils are formed. Rocks are weathered into small particles by wind, rain and frost, and the tiny particles are eroded by wind or water and deposited, often by flooding, into fertile plains and valleys.

▶ Look at the soil pictures in turn and ask the children if they can explain why they are different colours. Talk about the bedrock influencing the type of soil in an area. (For example red sandstone; chalk near the surface soil.)

▶ Talk about the different properties of the soils; that some, like the chalky soil, drain quickly, while others, like the heavy clay soil, hold water and become waterlogged. Different types of plants prefer different types of soil. Some plants like a heavy soil that retains water while others prefer a well-drained soil.

▶ Tell the children that soils also contain decaying organic materials.

Activities

▶ Bring in a tray of soil and ask the children to use a hand lens to look at the different particles. Look for evidence of decaying plant material (humus), small stones and so on. If you are sure the soil is 'clean', let the children feel the different textures, squeezing small amounts between their fingers and seeing how well they crumble.

▶ Compare the local soil with that from a different area. Is it the same colour? Does it feel the same? Is it stonier?

▶ Use different soils as pigments to create landscape pictures. If used like powder paint, different soils will give shades from black to yellow. These can be used to create subtle pictures that do not fade. Ask the children who might have used this technique thousands of years ago. Has anyone seen any cave paintings?

▶ Put a tray of fresh soil under a table lamp for a short time and let the children observe any small creatures brought to the surface by the warmth. Make sure the lamp is not too hot and that any creatures are otherwise undisturbed and returned to their natural habitat within a fairly short time.

▶ Shake a small amount of soil in a jar of water. Allow it to settle and observe the different layers produced. Humus will float at the top of the water while the rest of the soil will settle at the bottom of the jar in layers, according to the size of particle. Small clay particles will form the top layers, silt and sand the middle layers and then small stones and grit will be at the bottom.

▶ Ask groups of children to plan and carry out an investigation to find out which type of soil drains best.

▶ If you have an appropriate site in the school field or garden, help the children dig a profile to show the different layers in the soil. Follow photocopiable page 68 so the children know what to do and look for.

▶ Let the children use gravel, soils and sands to make a miniature landscape in a seed tray. They could try planting it with small plants such as cress or grass and moss.

PUDDLES AND FLOODS

Puddles, Flooded fields

Some soils are more likely to hold water, causing puddles to form – or in extreme cases, floods. Clay soils drain much more slowly than those of a more sandy or loamy nature, so they are more likely to have puddles and be muddy. It is possible to find puddles on a beach even though sand drains very quickly because at certain points the underlying rock may be very near the surface, preventing the water from draining away. Similarly, some moorlands may be quite boggy in places. Looking at the number of puddles and how quickly they disappear may be a guide to the type of soil in an area.

Discussing the photographs

▶ Talk about where the children usually find puddles in the local area after rain. Why do some puddles last longer than others? Some of the water may drain away and some may evaporate. On a slow draining soil the disappearance of the puddle will depend mainly on evaporation

▶ Look at the 'Puddles' photograph and discuss why the puddles might be there. The fields may be in an area of clay soil, which will hold the water. Also, the number of people walking on the ground will make it uneven and some parts more compacted (and so more water retentive) than others.

▶ Look at the picture of the flooded field. Floods like this may do an enormous amount of damage, drowning crops and sometimes washing away fertile topsoil. In other cases, such as in the Nile valley before the construction of the Aswan High Dam, agriculture is dependent on the annual floods bringing silt that makes the land fertile.

Activities

▶ Take the children to look at the school field after rain to find any puddles. Mark them on a simple map. Look again after about an hour. Are the puddles still in the same places? Are they the same size? See if the children can decide what type of soil the field is on by how fast the puddles disappear.

▶ Conduct an investigation to find out in which soil type puddles might last longest. Line two plastic colanders with cloth (J-cloth is useful). Put sand in one colander and clay in the other. Press down firmly and make a shallow depression in the centre of each. Pour measured amounts of water in each depression and leave the colanders to drain. Which puddle disappears fastest? Ask the children to record and explain their findings.

▶ Read the information about canal building on photocopiable page 69. Explain that some cheap and plentiful material had to be found that would prevent water draining away, so the bottom and sides of canals were lined with compacted clay. This proved so effective that the canals are still holding water to the present day, a hundred years or more later. Encourage the children to find out more about canals in this country.

NOTES ON THE PHOTOCOPIABLE PAGES

Word cards

PAGES 63–6

These cards contain some of the key words that the children will need to know and will find useful when learning about rocks and soils. They include:

▶ types and characteristics of rocks and soils, such as *slate, clay, porous*

▶ man-made building materials, such as *brick, cement, paving*

▶ words related to rock formations, such as *mountain, cliff, quarry.*

Read the words with the children to familiarise them with the key words of the unit. Ask the children which words they have heard before. Are there any words they don't understand?

Activities
▶ Spread the cards on the table and ask the children to find specific words as you call them out.
▶ Use the word cards as a word bank to help the children label pictures or to help them with their writing.
▶ Encourage the children to use the cards to compile a glossary for this topic.
▶ Use them to label samples of rock brought into the classroom.

How rocks are formed

PAGE 67

This sheet gives a simple explanation of how the three main types of rock are formed. The children could use it as a fact sheet as a basis to produce their own explanation or information texts.

Discussing the text
▶ Explain to the children that there are three main types of rock: sedimentary (those formed by layers of sediment), igneous (those formed by heat) and metamorphic (those formed by heat and pressure).
▶ Read the explanations one at a time and talk through each with the children in order to help them understand the processes involved.
▶ Can the children explain why some rocks are layered?
▶ Ask why some rocks contain crystals and others do not.
▶ Discuss how heat plays a part in forming rocks.
▶ What happens to rocks when they are subjected to wind, water or frost?

Activities
▶ Use the Internet or reference books to find out more about the three main types of rocks. Ask the children to draw diagrams to illustrate the processes.
▶ In groups, ask the children to examine a collection of rocks and try to decide which main group they belong to. Remind them to give reasons for their choices. Does everyone agree?

Taking a soil profile

PAGE 68

This sheet gives simple instructions on how to make a soil profile so that the children can observe at first hand the different layers in the soil, from topsoil down to bedrock, and fully appreciate that beneath all surfaces there is rock.

You may wish to prepare the soil profile in advance for the children to observe. Once dug, a sheet of perspex placed in font of the profile means that you have a longlasting resource. If possible, dig out the side of the hole opposite the profile to make a gentle slope. This will make the hole safer and the profile much easier for the children to see. Make sure the children understand the dangers of falling down the hole. It is better if they are organised in small groups to make their observations so that they can see without pushing and jostling.

Discussing the text
▶ Ask the children if they can explain what is meant by a soil profile. What would they expect to find in the top layer and what in the bottom? What they would expect to find if they dug down far enough? (Rock.)
▶ Read through the instructions for making their own soil profile and discuss where might be a sensible place to dig a profile in the school grounds. If you have a heavy soil, you may need help to dig.
▶ Look at the photograph of the soil profile again and ask the children to describe what they see. Can they give an explanation of the different colours?

Activities
▶ Take the children out in supervised groups and follow the instructions on the sheet.
▶ Look carefully at the profile and use plastic plant labels to mark the different layers.

▶ Let the children take a small sample from each layer and look at it under a hand lens. What differences are there?

▶ Ask the children to draw a detailed picture or map of the profile, labelling the layers. Let them use the photograph provided on the CD to help them distinguish layers.

▶ Compare the school profile with that in the photograph.

Building canals   PAGE 69

This is a brief history of how the canals were built in Victorian times and how clay was used to give the canals a waterproof lining. The children can extend the information provided through their own research.

Discussing the text
▶ Read the text together. Talk about canals as an important way of transporting heavy goods in Victorian times and how vital they were to industry.

▶ Emphasise the fact that they were dug without the aid of machinery, but by men using picks and shovels.

▶ Talk about how the clay had to be very firmly tramped down or *puddled* so that there were no weak spots through which the water could leak.

▶ Can the children tell you why canals are now rarely used for the transportation of heavy goods? How are they transported now?

▶ Talk about what canals are mainly used for today. Ask the children if they have been on a canal boat and to share their experiences.

Activities
▶ Ask the children to find the information in the text on why the men who built the canals were called 'navvies'. Then ask them to find out where the majority of them came from.

▶ Look at a map of the local area and find any canals marked on it.

▶ Organise a visit to a canal or a trip on a narrow boat. Ask the children to look carefully at the lock gates, then find out how they work. Why are they needed?

▶ Look at some powdered clay and some sand in a small dish under a magnifier. Note the difference in the size of the particles. Dampen each sample and rub gently to feel how the particles behave when water is added. Look again with a magnifier. How have the samples changed?

▶ Help the children to devise a fair test to compare how well sand and clay drain. Place filter papers in the bottom of three plastic funnels or tie a small piece of J-cloth over the end. Fill one funnel with sand, place a ball of clay in the second and pack clay firmly into the third. Pour a measured amount of water into each funnel. Which drains fastest? Explain your findings in terms of puddling clay.

Photograph © Corel

Rocks and soils word cards

slate

marble

granite

gravel

chalk

sand	clay

sandstone

pebble

porous

◖ S C H O L A S T I C
PHOTOCOPIABLE

Made materials word cards

brick

breeze-block

tile

concrete

cement

paving

◖SCHOLASTIC
PHOTOCOPIABLE

Formations word cards

quarry

mountain

rock face

rocky outcrop

field	cliff
moor	dale

valley

canyon

◪ SCHOLASTIC
PHOTOCOPIABLE

How rocks are formed

Sedimentary rocks

Rivers flowing down from hills and mountains to the sea take with them lots of sediment – tiny bits of sand and soil eroded as the river travels. These bits settle on the seabed and get squashed down until they are quite hard. Gradually, over millions of years, layers build up. You can see these layers in sections of hard rock that is no longer underwater. Sometimes, the bodies of dead animals are caught in the

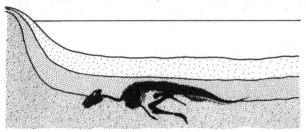

layers, and these turn into fossils. Fossils can often be found in sedimentary rocks such as sandstone and limestone.

Igneous rocks

Deep in the centre of the Earth, where it is very hot, rock is in a melted form called magma. Sometimes, the magma finds its way into cavities in the Earth's crust, where it can cool slowly to form rocks such as granite. These rocks contain crystals. The slower the rock cools, the bigger the crystals. When a volcano erupts, magma reaches the surface of the Earth. If that happens, the magma cools more quickly to form rocks such as lava and pumice.

Metamorphic rocks

These are rocks that were once sedimentary, igneous or old metamorphic rocks, but have changed. They are formed deep in the Earth when rock is subjected to great pressures and gets extremely hot (but not hot enough to melt it into magma). The sedimentary rock limestone is changed through heat and pressure into marble; mudstone or shale can be changed into slate.

Images © Soda

Taking a soil profile

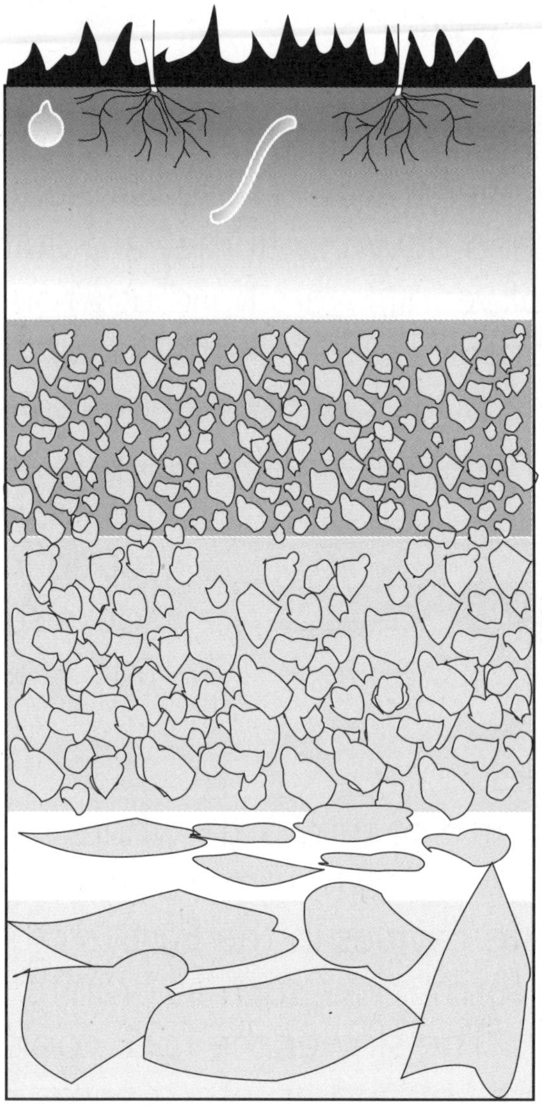

1. Choose an area of soil that has not been disturbed for some time.

2. Ask for permission to dig in the area.

3. Spread some bin bags where you are going to dig, to put the soil on.

4. Dig down until you reach rock, or about 1 metre.

5. Create at least one good straight side to the profile. Make the hole big enough to be able to see this side clearly.

6. Look for the dark layer at the top where organic matter has mixed with the soil. This is the most fertile layer. The soil will gradually change colour and become stonier until you reach the bedrock, which is the origin of the soil. The layers may be quite distinct in some areas.

7. If your hole/profile is in a place where it can be safely left, a large piece of Perspex can be placed against the side to preserve the profile for future work, otherwise make sure that the hole is safely filled in before leaving the site.

top, dark layer of fertile soil

lighter layer (sub-soil), lacking humus

layer including small stones

stonier layer, no organic material

underlying bedrock

Image © Soda

◾SCHOLASTIC PHOTOCOPIABLE

Building canals

During the early Victorian era, when heavy industry was developing at a fast rate, canals were the principal way of moving goods such as coal, iron and brick.

If a canal were to be dug today, powerful machinery would be used, but in those days men had to build the canals with hand tools. The workmen taking on this immense task would travel all over the country to work wherever a canal was being built. These workers were called 'navigators', or 'navvies', because they were cutting canals to open up new routes for trade. It was dirty and dangerous work and many men were killed in the process. During the construction of the Regent's Canal in London, for example, the banks collapsed and buried some of the men working there.

Construction

To begin building a canal, a deep trench was dug and the loosened soil taken up the banks in wheelbarrows. To stop water draining away, a method of waterproofing had to be found. A special clay mixture was spread thickly over the flat bottom and sloping sides of the trench. In some places, this mixture was up to three feet thick. It was then packed hard or 'puddled' so that it would become watertight. Often, the navvies did this with their feet, tramping up and down the trench. Sometimes, cattle or other large animals were driven down the floor of the trench. This compressed the clay and helped to seal any cracks to prevent leaks.

Canals were built as narrow as possible to minimise the amount of digging and lining material needed. Canal boats had to be built long and narrow to be able to use them, which is why they are usually called narrow boats.

Aqueducts

Puddled clay was also used to waterproof canal bridges, such as the one on the Bridgewater Canal where it crosses the River Irwell near Manchester. A masonry aqueduct was puddled with clay to carry the canal. Before the aqueduct was built, sceptical MPs called the builder, James Brindley, into the House of Commons to explain his theory. He took wet clay and buckets of water into their offices to prove that clay could indeed be made waterproof.

Image © Corel

LIGHT AND SHADOWS

Content and skills

This chapter links to unit 3F, 'Light and shadows', of the QCA Scheme of Work for science at Key Stage 2. The Light and shadows Resource Gallery on the CD-ROM, together with the teacher's notes and photocopiable pages in this chapter, can be used when teaching this unit.

As with the QCA Scheme of Work, this chapter builds on 'Light and dark' from Year 1. It helps children understand the relationships between light and shadows and learn about different light sources.

The teacher's notes contain background information about the resources and include ways of using them as a whole class, for group work or as individuals. A poem has been included in the photocopiable pages, which can be used as initial stimulation or as reinforcement of the ideas contained in the unit. Some of the activities link with other areas of the curriculum, such as geography, maths, art and English. Wherever possible, the activities encourage the children to ask questions and develop an enquiring approach to their learning.

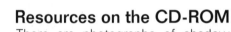

Resources on the CD-ROM

There are photographs of shadows in winter and summer, showing how shadows change in length according to the inclination of the Sun. Pictures of sundials illustrate how their designs have changed and how shadows were used to tell the time before mechanical clocks were invented.

A video clip shows a washing line and a child moving, and the consequent changes in their shadows. The clip also includes a short time-lapse sequence of a shadow moving clockwise around a shadow stick.

Photocopiable pages

The photocopiable pages in the book are also provided in PDF format on the CD-ROM and can be printed from there. They include:

▶ word cards containing essential vocabulary for the topic
▶ a classic poem
▶ a brief history of sundials
▶ a detailed chronology of the development of sundials and clocks.

Science skills

Skills such as observing, questioning, describing, finding out, sorting, sequencing, listening, speaking, reading, writing and drawing are involved in the activities suggested for the unit. For example, observing the change in shadows according to the angle and direction of the light source will help children understand the relationship between light and shadow. Looking at sundials and finding out how they work will help children understand how the measurement of time has evolved.

Photograph © Ross Whitaker/Soda

NOTES ON THE CD-ROM RESOURCES

MOVING SHADOWS

Video: Moving shadows

This video can help children to understand a number of concepts about shadows. It can be used to show that shadows are similar in shape to the object making them and that if the object moves, they move with it. (For example, a child running about on a sunny day, or a tree blowing in the wind.) The time-lapse sequence in the middle part of the film shows a shadow stick and its shadow moving clockwise, lengthening and shortening as it does so.

Discussing the video

▶ Watch the video together. Ask the children to watch how the shadows move as the washing and the child move about. Are the shadows recognisable? Are the shadows of each piece of washing always pointing in the same direction?

▶ Talk about the shadow stick. Explain that the film has been speeded up so that we can see a process that normally takes hours. Ask the children to look at which way the shadow moves around the stick and explain why it moves clockwise. (In the Northern Hemisphere, the Earth appears to rotate in an anti-clockwise direction, so the shadow moves clockwise.)

▶ Look at how the stick shadow changes in length and ask the children to explain why this happens. (As the Sun appears to climb in the sky, the shadows get shorter. When the Sun is at a lower angle, the shadows lengthen.)

▶ Look at the child's feet and notice how the shadow touches them.

Activities

▶ Investigate making shadows using different objects. Try using opaque objects, such as a book or a candle; translucent objects, such a plastic lunch box; and transparent things, such as a jar or magnifier. Use a light source and throw the shadows onto a screen or sheet of white card. Encourage the children to investigate how they can get the sharpest shadow (change the distances between object, light source and screen) or find out what happens if they change the height of the light source and so on (the shadow length will change).

▶ Ask the children to write a short explanation about how shadows are formed, making the relationship between light, object and shadow clear.

▶ Working in pairs, ask the children to draw silhouettes of each other using a bright light to throw a shadow onto large sheets of black paper pinned to the wall. Cut out the shape and mount this on white paper. Can the children recognise their friends from the silhouettes?

▶ Using a bright light, let the children investigate making shadows with their hands on a plain wall or screen. Do the shadows always look like their hands? Can they make shapes of animals using their fingers?

▶ Let the children experiment with making a Plasticine shape and bending it in different ways to show how the shape of the shadow also changes. Encourage them to shine the light from different angles.

▶ Read the poem 'My shadow' on photocopiable page 80, then ask the children to write their own poem about their observations of shadows moving.

SHADOWS

Winter shadow, Summer shadow

These images provide a good starting point for discussing shadows formed by the Sun as a light source. Children need to know how shadows are formed and recognise that they are similar in shape to the object forming them. They also need to understand that the angle and position of the light source will influence the length of the shadows and where they appear. The Earth's rotation means that the length and position of shadows change as the Sun apparently moves across the sky and changes its elevation during the day. The angle of the Earth's tilt relative to the Sun means that in the summer the Sun is more directly overhead than in winter: summer shadows are shorter than those that occur in the winter.

It is important to emphasise to children the danger of looking directly at the Sun.

Discussing the photographs

▶ Look at 'Winter shadow'. Ask the children if they can tell you what time of year it is. Can they explain their answer? (There are no leaves on the trees; snow is on the ground.)

▶ Ask the children to look at where the Sun is and where the shadow is. Point out that the Sun is behind the tree, and the tree blocking light from the Sun has caused the shadow.

▶ Notice the shape of the shadow and how it is very similar to that of the tree.

▶ Ask the children if shadows are always the same length. Talk about why shadows change during the day and explain that shadows are also longer in the winter than in the summer.

▶ Look at 'Summer shadow'. Ask the children what time of year this photograph was taken. How do they know? Where do they think the Sun was when the picture was taken? (Overhead.) Approximately what time of day do they think it may be? (Around midday.)

▶ Compare the length of shadow with that of the winter tree.

▶ Ask the children if they have noticed shadows anywhere else. Most will have seen their own shadows at some point. Some may have seen multiple shadows at a floodlit sport event. Why does this happen? (The floodlight in each corner of the pitch forms its own shadows.)

Activities

▶ Ask the children to compare the two photographs in detail.

▶ Go out into the playground together, fairly early on a sunny day, and look for shadows. Use chalk to mark some of the shadows formed by the buildings and objects such as bins and tall flowers. Look again later in the day and notice any changes in size or position of the shadows. Tell the children to make and record accurate measurements.

▶ Position one or two children in marked spots in the playground and draw their shadows. Again, go out later in the day and check for changes. If circumstances allow, use emulsion paint to fill in the shadows. This will eventually wear off, but last long enough for them to be revisited during the unit. Mark each painted shadow with the date and time of day.

▶ Take the children outside to walk round the school, keeping to the shadows. Go out again later in the day and see if you can still use the same route. Have the changing shadows made it necessary to go a different way?

▶ Use a lamp, a simple object and a screen to show how the height of the light source affects the length of the shadow.

SUNDIALS

Metal sundial, Stone sundial, Portable pillar sundial

Shadows can be used to tell the time of day. Each rotation of the Earth on its axis takes one day and makes it appear as though the Sun moves across the sky. In the northern hemisphere, shadows move clockwise during the day. However, the tilt of the Earth and its position in its orbit round the Sun means that the Sun's path appears to vary, very slightly, from day to day. Sundials overcome this by either positioning the gnomon (the rod that makes the shadow) at an angle parallel to the Earth's tilt or having the plate tilted in line with the Earth's latitude. If this type of sundial is moved from the place that it is set up for, it will no longer tell the time accurately. The divisions on the plate of a sundial are not equidistant, since the shadow is affected by the direction and the elevation of the light source (Sun) which both change during the course of the day. As the Sun appears to move during the day, the shadow cast by the gnomon, which must be oriented in a North/South direction, moves around the 'dial', giving an indication of the time of day. Sundials, of course, do not work at night.

Discussing the photographs

▶ Look at all three objects. Can the children tell you what they are?

▶ Explain that people used sundials to tell the time before clocks and watches. Discuss how, thousands of years ago, people noticed that shadows moved in a regular pattern through the day and that they could tell what time of day it was according to where the shadows lay.

▶ Explain that sundials became remarkably accurate as people found out more about the shape and tilt of the Earth and adjusted sundials according to latitude.

▶ Mention that only rich people could afford a sundial of their own, but eventually sundials were put on churches so that everyone could use them to tell the time.

▶ Explain that because of the shape of the Earth, the time differed from place to place, until a standard time was adopted country-wide.

▶ Explain that nowadays, sundials are mostly used as garden ornaments. Help the children to see how decorative the stone sundial is, where it is placed, and that it is engraved with the date 1905, after clocks were in common use.

▶ Look at the 'Portable pillar sundial' and explain that it is from the 17th century. Ask the children what they think it was used for. This type of sundial was small enough to be carried around. When pocket watches were first invented they were unreliable, and people still carried a portable sundial so that they could adjust their mechanical timepieces. Various types of portable sundials were developed, some including compasses to help in setting them up correctly in a North/South direction so that the Sun struck the gnomon correctly.

Activities

▶ Read and discuss 'Telling the time' on photocopiable page 77.

▶ Look again at the playground shadows made by the children. If they were made early and again later in the day, there will probably be a fairly large angle of change in the shadows. Ask the children how they could track the rate of movement.

▶ Place a shadow stick (gnomon) in a suitable sunny spot and mark the shadow it makes every hour on the hour. After the first three or four readings, ask the children if they can predict where the next shadow will fall.

▶ Next day, compare the shadow stick with a clock to see how accurate it is. What allowance would you need to make for British Summer Time?

▶ Watch the section of time-lapse footage in the 'Moving shadows' video that shows the shadow moving clockwise around the shadow stick.

▶ Experiment with a desk lamp and a simple object, such as an unlit candle stuck in Plasticine, to find a good way of making a clear shadow. Investigate how the shadow moves if the light source is moved around the object. What does this tell us about the apparent movement of the Sun?

▶ Ask the children to draw a diagram that can help explain how shadows are formed.

▶ Let them design and make simple sundials from materials found in the school or grounds.

▶ Find out if there are any sundials in the vicinity. Take photographs, if possible, and find out more about their history. There may be one at the local church.

▶ Look at a globe and show the children the lines of latitude. Ask the children to find out how latitude affects a sundial. For example, what happens to shadows on the equator?

▶ Ask the children to use the chronology on photocopiable pages 78–9 to find out more about sundials and write a short history.

NOTES ON THE PHOTOCOPIABLE PAGES

Word cards   PAGES 75–6

These cards contain some of the basic words and phrases the children will come across when learning about light and shadows. They include:

▶ words associated with light, such as *light source, direction, opaque*

▶ words associated with shadow formation, such as *Earth's axis, sundial, block*.

Read the cards with the children to familiarise them with the vocabulary.

Activities

▶ Spread the cards on the table and ask the children to find specific words

▶ Use them as a word bank to help the children with their writing.

▶ Begin a glossary with the words, and include any other topic vocabulary used in the unit.

Telling the time   PAGE 77

This information text provides an outline of the history of sundials.

Discussing the text

▶ Read the text and establish when sundials were first used and how they developed.

▶ Discuss why it is useful to know the time and how this has become increasingly important.

▶ Ask the children to tell you their ideas about how people knew the time of day before sundials were invented. How accurate could they be? Could they measure minutes and seconds? Did they need to?

▶ Why do we measure minutes and seconds? Can the children tell you instances where accuracy is important? For example, boiling an egg, using the microwave, timing races.

Activities
See 'Chronology of sundials', below.

Chronology of sundials

PAGES 78–9

This table provides more detailed information about the history of telling the time. It traces the development of using the Sun, and the Earth's movement around it, to track time, moving on up to developments in the 20th century.

The text will be a challenge, so take some time to read and explain it carefully.

Discussing the text
▶ Read through the chronology together. You will probably want to break this down into several reading chunks.

▶ Establish how long ago sundials were first used.

▶ Talk about how measuring time accurately became more important as civilisations developed and societies became more complex.

Activities
▶ Ask the children to find out about other timekeeping devices, such as water clocks and candle clocks.

▶ Look around and make a list of equipment that has its own built-in clock or timer, for example a video recorder, a microwave, a car and so on.

▶ Ask the children to find out about how 'time' is governed by the movements of the Earth, both its rotation on its axis and its orbit around the Sun. What is a year? What is a day? What is a month and so on?

My Shadow

PAGE 80

This classic poem highlights many aspects of work on shadows, for example that the child's shadow is the same shape as him and is only cast when there is a light source (Sun or candle). Close examination of the lines in the poem provides a good opportunity for children to explain these aspects in detail.

Some of the concepts and vocabulary are old-fashioned and unfamiliar, so you will need to read it a couple of times and explain these before the children work individually.

Discussing the poem
▶ Read through the poem together. What do the children think the poet means when he says that the shadow *goes in and out with me*? Relate it to work the children may have done observing their own shadows when out playing.

▶ Remind the children how shadows are shaped like the objects that make them.

▶ Ask them why the author says his shadow jumps into bed with him? Do they ever see their own shadows at night? Explain that the poem was written a long time ago and ask the children what they think would have been the light source.

▶ Ask what the poet is referring to when he says that the shadow grows or gets smaller.

▶ Why might the shadow disappear altogether? What is actually happening when the poet says the shadow *was fast asleep in bed* very early in the morning?

Activities
▶ Ask the children to write shadow poems of their own.

▶ Ask the children to illustrate one of the events in the poem. Make sure that they show the light source and shadow correctly, as well as ensuring that the shadow joins the object.

▶ Watch the 'Moving shadows' video to see how the shadows move and change. The children could write a poem about one of the sequences in the film.

Light word cards

transparent
opaque
translucent
shiny
light source
direction
light travels

SCHOLASTIC
PHOTOCOPIABLE

Shadow word cards

Earth's axis

rotation

lengthen

shorter

sundial

gnomon

formation

block

sharpest

■ SCHOLASTIC
PHOTOCOPIABLE

Telling the time

Thousands of years ago, people noticed that shadows moved in a regular pattern throughout the day, and that they could tell roughly what time of day it was according to where the shadows lay. They could tell whether it was early morning, midday or late afternoon, but not that it was quarter past three or ten minutes to nine – and, of course, it didn't work on cloudy days or at night.

There is evidence that the Maya people of Central America were using astronomical observations to mark days and months some 8000 or 9000 years BC. Around 3000BC, the Egyptians started using a calendar that had 365 days in a year.

Gradually, people learned more and more about the movement of the Earth around the Sun. Sundials became remarkably accurate as people found out about the shape of the Earth and made adjustments according to latitude.

Only rich people could afford a sundial of their own, but in AD650 the Pope ordered that sundials should be put on churches so that everyone could use them. They were very important for telling the time until clocks were invented, but because of the shape and rotation of the Earth, the shadows differed from place to place. Each town and city had its own regional time. In this country, it wasn't until the railway network was developed and timetables were produced that people needed to have a system that gave the same time everywhere in the country. This resulted in Greenwich Mean Time (using the line of zero longitude) being adopted throughout Great Britain.

Nowadays, when we nearly all have analogue and digital clocks at home and school, and watches that we can wear on our wrists, sundials are mostly used as garden ornaments. The passage of time is now measured very accurately according to the minute movement of atoms, rather than relying on the rotation of the Earth.

Chronology of sundials

Here are some selected dates in the development of sundials and solar astronomy. For more information go to www.sundialsoc.org.uk.

9000–8000BC	The Maya, in Central America, make astronomical records from observations of the Sun and stars.
1400BC	Stonehenge, which is aligned with the Sun, begins to look like it does today.
520–510BC	Anaximander introduces the sundial to Greece. It was previously used in Mesopotamia, Egypt and China. He also produces a cylindrical model of the Earth.
480–470BC	The Greek philosopher Oenopides calculates that the axis of the Earth is tipped over by 24 degrees.
270–260BC	Aristarchus of Samos (a small island near Turkey) challenges Aristotle's theory by asserting that the Sun is at the centre of the solar system and the planets revolve around it. He estimates the distances of the Moon and (wrongly) the Sun from the Earth.
164BC	Pliny records that a sundial is properly set up for the first time in Rome, and the Romans begin to divide daylight into hours.
10BC	Augustus erects a monumental sundial in Rome: the 15-metre stone obelisk gnomon, brought from Egypt. It was surrounded by numerous lines for the hours, days and months.
AD664	The Synod of Whitby determines the inaccuracies in the current calendar. The term *Anno Domini* ('in the year of our Lord') is introduced.
c650	Pope Sabinianus commands that sundials should be placed on churches to show the hour of the day.
670–679	The Venerable Bede (an English monk and scholar who had attended the Synod of Whitby) writes about the calendar, marine tides and the shape of the Earth. He also gives an accurate table of shadow lengths.
c700	The oldest surviving Anglo-Saxon sundials in England are built.
1200–1300	Returning crusaders bring Islamic knowledge of the polar gnomon and many different dial types to Europe.
1276	Chinese astronomer Zhou Kung sets up a 12-metre gnomon for measuring the sun's shadow.

Image © Ingram Publishing

READY RESOURCES ▶▶ S C I E N C E

SCHOLASTIC
PHOTOCOPIABLE

Chronology of sundials (cont)

1517	Nicholas Kratzer comes to England from Austria to be horologist to King Henry VIII. He later makes several famous dials and is painted by Hans Holbein.
1606	Elias Allen, one of the greatest dial and scientific instrument makers of the era, is established near Fleet Street, London.
1655	Gian Domenico Cassini builds the great sundial in Bologna cathedral.
1675	The Greenwich Observatory is founded by King Charles II. John Flamsteed is the first Astronomer Royal.
1724	Jai Singh, Rajah of Jaipur, builds his great sundials in India.
1750	The Greenwich Meridian is established at its current position by James Bradley. It had initially been 20.4 metres further west.
1756	JJ de Lalande designs the oldest analemmatic dial still in existence, in Brou churchyard, France.
1847	Railway time (by now used by most railway companies) is declared "a dangerous innovation" in the *Times* newspaper. Clocks are now in general use.
1852	Exeter Cathedral clock is put forward 14 minutes to read London Time. There are still many places using local time, for example Plymouth and Oxford, plus rural areas.
1872	Mrs Gatty publishes *The Book of Sundials*, giving examples of many dials and their mottoes.
1880	(Aug) The Definition of Time Act finally establishes Greenwich time as the basis for civil timekeeping throughout Great Britain.
1884	(Oct) The International Meridian Conference in Washington, DC, sets the Prime Meridian through Greenwich and defines the standard time zones. It also establishes the mean solar day, and voices a desire to extend the use of the decimal system.
1900	The last French railway stations abandon the use of heliochronometers for setting their clocks.
1924	The BBC begins the world's first public time broadcast by transmitting the time 'pips', having started with a piano playing the Westminster chimes two years earlier.
1974	Robert Gundlach is awarded a US patent for a shadowless sundial; this design has some similarities to the later CD dial.
1981	Boon obtains a US patent for a digital sundial. It is later improved by RL Kellogg.
1984	The second is redefined based on atomic rather than Earth-rotation principles.

My Shadow

I have a little shadow that goes in and out with me,
And what can be the use of him is more than I can see.
He is very, very like me from the heels up to the head;
And I see him jump before me, when I jump into my bed.

The funniest thing about him is the way he likes to grow –
Not at all like proper children, which is always very slow;
For he sometimes shoots up taller like an india-rubber ball,
And he sometimes gets so little that there's none of him at all.

He hasn't got a notion of how children ought to play,
And can only make a fool of me in every sort of way.
He stays so close beside me, he's a coward you can see;
I'd think shame to stick to nursie as that shadow sticks to me!

One morning, very early, before the sun was up,
I rose and found the shining dew on every buttercup;
But my lazy little shadow, like an arrant sleepy-head,
Had stayed at home behind me and was fast asleep in bed.

Robert Louis Stevenson

Image © Ross Whitaker\Soda

◖ SCHOLASTIC
PHOTOCOPIABLE